THE 7 SECRETS OF SUCCESSFUL BUSINESS NETWORKING

SECRET 1: THERE ARE 5 NETWORKER CATEGORIES

SECRET 2: TAKE A "NAPP" AND GET MORE REFERRALS

SECRET 3: LOOKING INSIDE BEFORE GOING OUTSIDE

SECRET 4: NETWORKERS ARE MADE, NOT BORN

SECRET 5: HELP YOURSELF BY HELPING OTHERS

SECRET 6: UNITED WE STAND, DIVERSIFIED WE CONQUER

SECRET 7: YOU CAN'T CATCH A FISH WITH A TORN NET

SUCCESSFUL BUSINESS NETWORKING

Successful Business Networking

Frank J. De Raffele Jr.
Edward D. Hendricks

Successful Business Networking

Copyright © 1998 by Frank J. De Raffele Jr. and Edward D. Hendricks

All rights reserved. Printed in the United States of America. No part of this book may be used or reproduced, stored or transmitted in any manner whatsoever without written permission from the Publisher, except in the case of brief quotations embodied in critical articles and reviews.

ISBN 1-886284-12-1

Library of Congress Catalog Card Number 97-77508

First Edition

ABCDEFGHIJK

Published by

Chandler House Press

335 Chandler Street
Worcester, MA 01602
USA

President
Lawrence J. Abramoff

Publisher/Editor-in-Chief
Richard J. Staron

Vice President of Sales
Irene S. Bergman

Editorial/Production Manager
Jennifer J. Goguen

Book Design
Bookmakers

Cover Design
Janet Amorello

Chandler House Press books are available at special discounts for bulk purchases. For more information about how to arrange such purchases, please contact Irene Bergman at Chandler House Press, 335 Chandler Street, Worcester, MA 01602, or call (800) 642-6657, or fax (508) 756-9425, or find us on the World Wide Web at www.tatnuck.com.

Chandler House Press books are distributed to the trade by

National Book Network, Inc.
4720 Boston Way
Lanham, MD 20706
(800) 462-6420

DEDICATION

FRANK J. DE RAFFELE JR.

First, I would like to dedicate this book to the two ladies who are the loves of my life. Without my wife, Crystal, and daughter, Jacqueline, none of what I do would be worthwhile or have meaning. It was not until I was married and had a daughter that I knew the true meaning of the word "Joy." A word that was never part of my vocabulary is now at the center of my spirit.

Second, I would like to dedicate this book to the rest of my immediate family. To my Mom and Dad who have led by example and shown me the true meaning of Networking. It is not something you do but something you become. It is a way of life. My sisters, Greta and Sandy, whose laughter, love and craziness I can't imagine living without.

Third, I would like to dedicate this book to all of my Networking Associates, especially those in my Primary and Secondary Networks. This book and the system within it are the result of all the experiences and time spent with those who have helped me.

Special Thank Yous

Dr. Ivan Misner, the guru of modern day networking. His knowledge, wisdom and never-ending ability and desire to give, I admire, respect and wish to emulate.

Lance Mead, Todd Hallinger, Patti Salvucci, Michael Brathwaite and Bob Staskel: For all your help, encouragement and great ideas over the years.

Marsha Rozales Gordon, President of the Southern Dutchess Chamber of Commerce.

John G. Tarleteon, President of the Poughkeepsie Area Chamber of Commerce.

Ed Hendricks, my S.B.N. partner—thanks for believing in me.

EDWARD D. HENDRICKS

Several years ago I received a very special award, one which I had a multitude of people to thank for assisting me in achieving it. The day I received the award, I made the following announcement: "I have so many people to thank that I started to make a list of names, but the only

DEDICATION

paper I could find that was long enough to contain all of the names was a roll of toilet paper. This morning as I thought about facing all of you in public, I became so nervous that I was forced to use the paper." In putting this book together, I face a similar conundrum—too many people to thank, and not enough space to do it in.

At the risk of upsetting all of those who have helped me in this endeavor, let me point out for special thank yous my wife, Betty, for all of her insights, hard work and willingness to put up with me. To Dick Staron, my publisher, editor and friend. And to Frank De Raffele who made the dream come true.

CONTENTS

INTRODUCTION		xxv
PURPOSE AND OVERVIEW OF SUCCESSFUL BUSINESS NETWORKING		xxxix
PART I	**GETTING STARTED**	**1**
1	NETWORKING WHYS AND WHEREFORES	3
	Five Ways to Market Your Business	10
2	WHAT IS NETWORKING?	13
	Doing What Comes Naturally	13
	Business Networking	14
	Networking Is Marketing	15
	Let's Get Physical	18
	Sometimes Bad Things Happen to Good People	20
3	YOU CAN'T AFFORD NOT TO NETWORK	23
	Time Is Your Most Precious Commodity—Trade It Well	23
	Climbing the Net of Success. . . No Ladders Needed	25
	Need It, Want It, Want to Buy or Sell It. . .	26

PART II ORGANIZATION **29**
Secret 1: There Are 5 Networker Categories

4 TAKING INVENTORY 31
Networking Goals 31
You Know More People than You Know 34
Your Five Networker Categories 35
Write 'Em Down 37
Make Sure You've Been Honest 45

5 NETWORKER'S DAILY ORGANIZER 47
Organizing and Operating Effectively 47
Networking Associates Address Book 50
Prioritized "To Do" List 61
Responsibility Note Pads 66
Real Life Appointment Schedule 68
Short- and Long-Term Goals Master Sheet 71
Various Calendars 77
    Annual Calendar 77
    Dates to Remember 79
    Quarterly 82
    Monthly Calendar 87

PART III EVALUATION **89**
Secret 2: Take a "NAPP" and Get More Referrals

6 EVALUATE YOUR NETWORKERS 91
Networker Associate Participation Program (NAPP) 91
What Have You Been Getting, If Anything? 92

Four Types of Help	92
Three Levels of Referrals	95
Simple Referral	95
Compound Referrals	97
Complex Referrals	98
The Primary-Complex Relationship	99
Chart Your Referrals	100

PART IV   RESEARCH   105
Secret 3: Looking Inside before Going Outside

7   TAKE A LOOK IN THE MIRROR   107

Habit 1—Be Proactive	109
Habit 2—Begin with the End in Mind	110
Habit 3—Put First Things First	111
Habit 4—Think Win/Win	111
Habit 5—Seek First to Understand, Then to be Understood	113
Habit 6—Synergize	114
Habit 7—Balanced Self-Renewal	115

8   FIND OUT WHICH NETWORKERS ARE MISSING   117

Your Primary "Net" Has Holes, Big Ones	117
Rescue the Networkers that You Do Have	121

PART V   SKILLS DEVELOPMENT   125
Secret 4: Networkers Are Made, Not Born

9   THE TRAITS OF SUCCESSFUL NETWORKERS   127

Networker Attributes	131
Additional Traits of Superior Networkers	136
Be a Silly Goose	138

SUCCESSFUL BUSINESS NETWORKING

10 DEVELOPING YOUR NETWORKING SKILLS — 141

Networking Is Not a Full Time Job—It's a Way of Life — 141
Educate, Train and Nurture Your Sales Force — 142
Don't Get Mixed Up by Mixers — 159
Networking Tools — 161
    Business Cards — 162
    Name Badge — 167
    Your Marketing Button — 167
    Personal Referral Card — 169
    Breath Neutralizers — 171
    The Rule of "7s" — 172
Different Types of Networking (Marketing) — 175

11 INTROVERT-EXTROVERT—DOES IT MATTER? — 181

How Introverts Act — 182
How Introverts Feel and Think — 183
How Extroverts Act — 184
How Extroverts Feel and Think — 185
A Self Evaluation — 186
Out of Your Comfort Zone — 193

12 LISTEN TO OTHERS IF YOU WANT TO BE HEARD — 197

10 Techniques of a Good Listener — 198

13 LEARNING TO TALK GOOD — 203

How to be P.R.E.P.A.R.E.D. — 204
    P = Plan — 204
    R = Rehearse — 206
    E = Edit — 208
    P = Psyche Yourself Up — 210
    A = Accept Your Uniqueness and Accentuate Your Strengths — 212
    R = Referrals Are Your Goal — 213

E = Evaluations Can be Helpful	214
D = Dress for Success	215

PART VI   NETWORK SALES & MARKETING — **217**
Secret 5: Help Yourself by Helping Others

14   WORK YOUR NETWORKS SINCERELY — 219
Move 'em Up — 219

15   TURN YOUR NETWORKERS AND CUSTOMERS INTO RAVING FANS — 233

16   ELEMENTS OF A BROAD-BASED MARKETING CAMPAIGN — 239

Elements Of Marketing	239
Marketing Methods	244
Strategic Positioning Options	253
Marketing Advice	254
10 Techniques to Get More Business	256
Some Final Thoughts about Marketing	258

17   60 PLUS SECRETS OF MARKETING — 261

PART VII   OPEN NEW MARKETS — **273**
Secret 6: United We Stand, Diversified We Conquer

18   REFERRAL GROUPS, CHAMBERS AND ASSOCIATIONS — 275

Referral Groups	276
Chambers of Commerce	277
Professional and Trade Associations	284
The Ten Commandments of Association Networking	288

XVI   **SUCCESSFUL BUSINESS NETWORKING**

19	INTRA-NETWORKING	289
	Cross-selling—an Elusive Goal	289

PART VIII   MAINTENANCE   **293**

Secret 7: You Can't Catch a Fish with a Torn Net

20	NETWORKING TOOLS: NO-TECH	295
	Keeping in Touch the Old-fashioned Way	295
	If You Want to Keep in Touch, Stay in Touch	299
21	NETWORKING TOOLS: LOW-TECH	299
	Database Generated Letters	300
	Newsletters	300
	Broadcast Faxes	302
	Put Your Words in Action	304
22	NETWORKING TOOLS: HIGH-TECH	305
	Networking in the 21st Century	305

PART IX   APPENDIX   **309**

23	TEST YOUR SKILLS	311
	Test Answers	317
24	NETWORKING STORIES OF THE FAMOUS AND NOT SO FAMOUS	321
	Make Yourself Memorable	321
	Win Friends and Influence People	322
	Let Other People Help You to the Top	323
	Remember the Little People	324
	Don't Be Afraid to Ask	324
	Networking Is a Universal Endeavor	325
25	THE ABCs OF NETWORKING	327

FOREWORD

We are not teaching the next generation of business professionals anything about building their business through networking or word-of-mouth marketing! Virtually no academic books on business or marketing focus on this area. Consequently, we are graduating scores of young people with bachelor's and graduate degrees in business and marketing and not giving them one iota of training in an area that almost all business practitioners agree is one of the most critical to the success of any enterprise.

We no longer live on *Little House on the Prairie*. We do not know all of the neighbors, not to mention most of the local people in the business community. Add to the equation our fascination with all that is technological and our growing propensity to "cocoon" from the outside world, and you have a picture of the emerging business professional that hasn't been trained in how to network and yet is entering a world that requires a greater and greater need to acquire these skills if they wish to build their business on the foundation of referrals.

A structured networking program works by putting you in touch with many other business professionals on a regular basis and in a positive environment. A structured networking program is also personally empowering; it's one of the few things that you, or someone who works for you, can do that directly effects your success.

Why wait for people to walk in your door? Why sit idly, hoping that your existing clients or customers will refer you to others? With a structured networking program, you don't have to wait for the results of your last PR campaign to kick in. Networking gives you control and allows you to take ownership for the business development of your business. Such a program has worked for millions of people in all types of businesses and will work for you as well.

Frank and Edward have tackled this challenge and have written an excellent book that can help anyone become a better networker. I have worked with tens of thousands of business professionals in helping them to develop successful networking programs. I can categorically state that if you follow the ideas outlined in this book, you will develop your networking expertise and enhance your abilities to build a word-of-mouth based business through networking. *Successful Business Networking* is all about building your business by developing relationships and working with your contacts. Frank and Edward do a tremendous job of showing you how to do that effectively. I am sure you will learn many important things about networking by reading this book. I know I have.

Ivan R. Misner, Ph.D.

Dr. Ivan Misner is the Founder and CEO of Business Network International (BNI), the largest referral marketing organization in the world. He has also authored four books on networking and word-of mouth marketing, including *The World's Best Known Marketing Secret* and *Business by Referral*.

PREFACE

This book is not only about networking; this book is the result of networking.

The story starts with our publisher, Dick Staron, who, several years ago, was employed by another publishing company. At that time Dick published a book written by Ford Harding, a friend of Ed Hendricks, one of the authors of this book. Shortly after publishing Ford's book, Dick became editor-in-chief at Macmillan Publishing Company in New York. He told Ford that he was looking for new authors of business books. Ford suggested that he call Ed Hendricks. Within a matter of weeks Ed was writing a book (*The Insider's Guide to Consulting Success*, 1997 Macmillan), and he also referred Dick to another member of his network, Ron Karr. Ron was commissioned by Dick to write a book as well.

While all of this was going on, Dick's family was living in Massachusetts while Dick was working in New York City. He mentioned this fact to Ed, who told Ron that Dick would like to find a publishing position in Massachusetts to be closer to his family. One day Ron told his in-laws about his publisher, Dick Staron, who was looking for a job in Massachusetts. As it turned out, Ron's in-laws owned a dry cleaning company across the street from a bookstore, Tatnuck Bookseller. The owner of Tatnuck Bookseller, Larry Abramoff, utilized the services of this dry cleaning company and happened to mention to the owners one day that he was thinking about expanding his operations to include book publishing. Well, you can guess the rest. Ron Karr's in-laws told Larry that their son-in-law had written a book which Dick Staron had published and that Dick was seeking to relocate from New York City. Ron told Dick about Larry, the two of them met, and *voila*, a marriage made in heaven.

Once Dick got on board as head of publishing at Chandler House Press (the publishing arm of Tatnuck Bookseller), he got back in touch with Ed Hendricks to talk about ideas for new books. Through his participation in the National Speakers Association, Ed had had an opportunity to do some training programs with a guy named Frank De Raffele, who just happened to have an idea for a book about business networking. Ed and Frank approached Dick with the idea, and you are holding the result of that meeting in your hand.

In this book you will learn about the five categories of networkers and the three levels of referrals. This book is proof that the system we will teach you really does work. We hope you will enjoy the fruits of our effort and that you will contact us with any comments or suggestions you might have for improving either the book or our system.

Edward D. Hendricks

Frank J. De Raffele Jr.

INTRODUCTION

FRANK J. DE RAFFELE JR.

When I think back on my childhood, one of the recurring memories is of my parents helping people: My mother helping her many friends at the school or the church, and my father helping other businessmen in the community get their own businesses started or assisting them in making decisions about starting their own businesses. As you read this book, it will be stated very clearly that the only true prerequisite for being an effective and successful networker is to be a giving person that enjoys helping others. If you give of yourself to others, that positive energy will be returned back to you many times over, and as this book will show, in dollars. My parents have always been very giving people. They committed and gave to each other in marriage, to their children in parenting and to others in the community throughout their lives. When you are brought up like this you can't help but find the joy in giving to others as well. Both of my sisters feel the same way. The times they are happiest is when they are giving of themselves to other people.

I started my first business when I was 19 and in college. My good friend and karate instructor at that time, Lee Montroy, wanted to start his own karate school. Lee was a great friend and a person who gave to me more than I could ever repay. When he expressed his interest in having his own karate school someday, I made it my mission to make that happen for him. I have always been very entrepreneurial and enjoyed the challenge and excitement of starting a new business. I began to map out ideas for a karate school and all the logistics it would take to get one up and running. I sat down with Lee and laid out what I had figured. He was impressed and a little shocked at the work I had dedicated to this project without him even asking. He proposed that I become his partner and we got things going. I created a logo with the help of my father, designed letterhead, a sign, and flyers and put together a marketing plan that involved the local Burger King and Ground Round Restaurants. We had our grand opening and we were up and running. At the grand opening I was able to see how proud and happy Lee was about owning his own business. That was enough for me. I wasn't concerned about making a dime from that business. I was just happy to have been able to help him.

After a couple of years I graduated from college, Lee continued his school and I faded out, allowing him to have his own business. Is this an example of networking? You better believe it. We built a relationship into a partnership that made money. That is the ultimate goal of business networking, to make money.

After I graduated from Syracuse University I still had the entrepreneurial bug. I couldn't go to work for anyone else. I had to own my own business. I had graduated with a degree in Speech Communications and Telecommunications, so I was hoping to do something in the area of video production. When I interviewed at companies, I was offered sales positions. I wanted to produce and direct. When I realized this wasn't going to happen, it became apparent to me that owning my own business was more important to me then being in the television production industry. It didn't matter what I did. I just wanted to do something I enjoyed. I decided to get a part time job at night to pay the bills and pursue my own business during the day.

I became a personal trainer at a health club during the afternoon and evening and started a video production company that specialized in producing video brochures for resorts. I had been looking in the *New York Times Magazine* one weekend and saw all these ads in the back of it for resorts and spas. I thought, "Wouldn't it be great if they had videos to show off their resorts to interested people?" *Voila*, a business! I started making phone calls and selling the idea. My first account was Weight Watchers Resorts & Spas in California. During this time I was also letting people at the health club know that I was in the process of getting my own company up and running. As I networked with people at the club I made some nice connections and got a couple of jobs from members who owned companies and wanted some video work done.

When I produced the Weight Watchers Resorts & Spas video I came up with the idea of producing a Weight Watchers Exercise Program video series. I spoke with the manager of the health club I was working at and asked him to work with me on designing the programs for the videos. We decided that instead of only submitting a proposal to this one company, we might as well approach several fitness companies. We ended up with a licensing agreement with Marcy Fitness Products in California. We produced 27 videotapes that instructed people on many different training programs for specific fitness goals such as: Improve Your Running, Reduce Your Golf /Tennis Elbow Pain, Body Sculpt Your Legs & Buttocks, etc. We produced the videos and they were selling well, but before long, Marcy Fitness Products was not doing well. Within 24 months they filed Chapter 11 and were sold to a bigger publicly owned company, and their fitness equipment was off the market. Our training tapes were based on their fitness equipment so we found ourselves with a load of obsolete tapes.

I decided to reinvest in myself and one of my true loves, karate. I started a martial arts school in Scarsdale, New York. After building up the school over a few years and developing a strong reputation in the area, I started speaking to youths about believing in yourself and living your life by the fundamental principle and values of the martial arts. I met a number of parents, teachers and community leaders during my speaking engagements, connections which led to my being asked to put together a program on starting and running your own business for local entrepreneurs. I developed a strong reputation of working with adults who wanted to be self-employed. I was teaching them how to take their dreams and develop them into profitable businesses by meeting the right people and developing these relationships to make things happen.

INTRODUCTION

During this time I got involved in my first referral group. I walked into the first meeting of a Business Network International chapter and said, "What a great concept." Since that time, one thing has lead to another and I now have opened, or assisted in the opening of, referral groups around the country. As I began to work with companies on leadership and teamwork development, I also started working with them on increasing their business through word-of-mouth marketing, networking and referrals.

I joined the National Speakers Association to enhance my speaking, training and consulting business. I became a board member for the New York Tri-State Chapter and met Ed Hendricks. As Ed and I built our relationship, we spoke of networking; then Ed mentioned our idea of a networking book to his publisher, and this book was born.

If you have followed this whole sequence of events, not to mention my life story, you can see that I have been networking my whole life. It was taught to me by watching my parents and has benefited me by all the connections I have made to this point. During the last few years, I have begun working on ways to take the happenstance out of networking and develop it into a system that can help anyone to achieve their goals quicker, easier and better than they ever expected. Ed and I have developed this system and put it in this book so everyone who is interested in learning it can achieve greater success. Networking is about helping people. I can think of no better way for me to help people become more effective networkers than by writing this book and by conducting seminars to help them take the knowledge they have learned and actually apply it and make it work. I have learned through experience that in contrast to the old saying, "Knowledge is power," it is not. "Knowledge is potential power." For knowledge to become power, you must have a system that can put knowledge into action. This book is the system. Read this book. Digest the information. Then, "Just Do It!"

EDWARD D. HENDRICKS

"It's not what you know. It's who you know." If I had a nickel for every time my mother repeated that phrase to me when I was growing up, I'd be a rich man today. As a child, of course, I doubted the wisdom of everything my parents had to say and was convinced that the way to get ahead in life was by getting good grades in school, going to college and that then, somehow, miraculously, the fabled Yellow Brick Road to success would appear before me. As I got older, however, I came to realize just how true my mother's words are. I'm certainly not saying that education doesn't matter, but after nearly 40 years in the work world, I have met more than my share of well-educated people who were stuck on the bottom rungs of the ladder and more than a few "dummies" who had climbed to the top because of the help they received along the way.

In my own case, I'd like to think it was a little of both—brain-power and contacts—which helped me to succeed. But for me education was the easy part—making contacts was far more difficult. As a truly shy and introverted person, making friends wasn't easy. Hopefully this book will ease the process for you.

Throughout my early years I was a very sickly child. As such, I tended quite naturally to become somewhat of a "Mama's Boy." I hated parties (and to a large extent still do), and I was certainly not the most popular kid in school. I was blessed with an ability to do well on tests, and graduated from elementary school and high school near the top of my class. I was so shy, however, and considered myself to be such a poor speaker that, as the saying goes, "I couldn't lead a group in silent prayer." After graduating from high school I made a conscious effort to break out of my shell when I went off to college. Unfortunately, I probably could have chosen a more productive way of doing so because after the first year, I was given the choice of either joining the military (this was during the Vietnam era) or going to jail. Since I don't look good in stripes, I chose the military. It was during my four years in the service that my life really turned around. I spent the first year aboard a ship sailing back and forth across the Pacific Ocean, and the second year on an isolated duty station on the island of Iwo Jima. At the time these two duty stations fit my personality perfectly. I didn't have to meet many new people, and I could get by on just what was expected of me.

During my third year in the service, however, I was assigned to a station in New York City. One night a friend of mine in the service asked me to go ice skating with him in Central Park. While we were there, knowing how shy and bashful I was, he bet me a soft drink that I couldn't meet two girls (one for him and one for me). Knowing I would lose the bet, but figuring soft drinks weren't all that expensive, I accepted the challenge. Within the first few minutes of stepping out onto the ice, I spotted a cute blonde who just happened to be there with another girl. I skated by and smiled at the blonde, and she smiled back. I'd like to say my heart leapt for joy, but more accurately, I developed a sinking feeling in the pit of my stomach! Now I was committed to making a fool of myself! Over the course of the next four hours (yes, four hours!), I continuously positioned myself where I was sure the blonde could see me, and I could see her. I continued to smile at her (by this point, she probably thought I had rictus, and I was rapidly approaching frostbite status). Nevertheless, she continued to smile back. Finally, the last skating session of the night was announced, and it was now or never. I was so afraid that I chose never. Fate (or the blonde) had other ideas. Just as I was about to give up, the blonde fell down right in front of me. I skated over and helped her up. I asked if she would like a cup of hot chocolate, and said that I noticed that she was there with a friend. I asked if her friend wanted to join us. My military buddy then came over, and the four of us went inside to warm up. The rest, as they say, is history! I won the soft drink and the blonde's heart. We were married less than a year later.

My wife, Betty, was and is a very popular person. She had a lot of friends, both socially and at work. She saw something in me that I couldn't recognize in myself, that I have the ability to make people feel good about themselves. This desire to want to help other people is the cornerstone of networking.

Networking is not about filling up your address book or collecting business cards. It is about wanting to help other people. In doing so, those other people tend to remember you and want to help you when an opportunity arises to do so.

When I was first discharged from the service, I really had no idea what I wanted to do. I took the first job that came along as a file clerk at a welding company. I was still extremely shy, but I did enjoy helping other people. One of the people I really liked, but didn't necessarily go out of my way to be friendly with, happened to be the secretary to the vice president of marketing. Within six months of my joining the firm, it underwent a reorganization, and rather than finding myself out on the street, I leap-frogged several levels in the company's organizational chart and took over my boss's job. Six months later, I was promoted to his boss's job. I was young enough and foolish enough to think that the higher-ups in the company recognized me as a rising star just because I was me. I learned the truth a few weeks later at a dinner meeting with one of the other department heads who, after a few drinks, took me aside and told me how lucky I was to have the executive vice president's secretary pulling strings for me to get me the promotions.

Not long after this, I received a call from a furniture company asking me to come in for an interview. I had no idea how they had gotten my name, but when I sat down with the head of human resources, I learned that his secretary was a friend of the secretary at the welding company. She had given my name to her friend when she had learned that the furniture company was expanding its operations. Because I came so highly recommended, I was offered the job as contracts manager at significantly more money than I had been making. Within six months I was asked to become regional sales manager for the Southeastern United States. Imagine that! Me, a bashful, shy Mama's Boy—a sales manager! I had never been a salesperson in my life! Yet here I was not only selling, but managing a sales force. This was all thanks to being nice to that secretary at the welding company. Maybe my mother was right, "It's not what you know. It's who you know." I was practically giddy with the prospect. In hindsight, giddy is not the right word—I was nutso! Here I was, a high school graduate with two young children making far more money than my milkman father had ever even dreamed about! It was too good to last.

I became totally self-absorbed and one-by-one began to burn my bridges behind me. I didn't have time to want to help other people, but I expected everyone to want to do things for me. I exceeded all of my sales goals, but my personal life became a shambles. I soon quit my job and retreated to the only thing I knew—I went back in the service.

I was given promises of a chance to further my education and possibly even attend law school through the military. I signed on the dotted line. Instead of law school, however, I was stationed on an ocean-going search-and-rescue tugboat. I never knew I could get so seasick! I was discharged a year later with no job, but with a wife, two children, a puppy and a parakeet. I was discharged back to North Carolina, which is where we were living when I went back into the service. We had squandered all of the money I had made from my previous job, and had total assets of about $35. I went to look for a job.

The first place I tried was the Sheriff's Department. I had no background in law enforcement, but several of my relatives had been police officers. Because I was a discharged veteran, the Sheriff of Mecklenburg County, North Carolina, took pity on me, and I started work the next day as a deputy sheriff. My wife was not thrilled. Her grandfather had been a corrections officer in New York State and was killed during a prison break. After many "discussions" she convinced me that I should consider going back to college. In other words, she gave me a choice— it was either her and the kids, or the sheriff's department. I applied and was accepted at the University of North Carolina at Charlotte.

As I said previously, I may not be real bright, but I can take tests. On the basis of my test scores, I was awarded a full scholarship to UNCC, and ultimately graduated *summa cum laude* with both a Bachelor of Arts and a Bachelor of Science degree.

During my time at the University I clearly recalled the importance of other people in helping me to get ahead. Even though I was still very shy, I forced myself to join a fraternity and to become active in student government. By my senior year I had managed to get all of the fraternities and sororities on campus to support me, and I was elected student body president. Here I was, older than the other students, a discharged military veteran, and a former law enforcement officer, and I was elected to a position of prominence at a time when college campuses were in revolt against the Vietnam War. I was not elected because of my intelligence, but because I really wanted this position and tried to help my fellow students in any way I could. They responded by voting for me in the campus elections.

As student body president I served as a member of the Board of Trustees of the University. Now I was in the big leagues! Board members included the mayor's brother, the congressman's campaign chairperson, and other movers and shakers in North Carolina business and politics. I was just old enough for the other trustees to accept me as a peer and young enough for them to want to look out for me. It was a great relationship.

After graduating from UNCC, I was awarded an academic fellowship to the State University of New York at Albany. I went into culture shock! I was no longer big man on campus and really missed that good old southern hospitality. Once again I withdrew into a shell and made no effort to get involved on campus or to meet people. I struggled through school and managed to get my Master's Degree in Criminal Justice. I applied for a position through the Law Enforcement Assistance Administration (LEAA) to work on a grant through the state of Connecticut. I got the job because that Sheriff down in Mecklenburg County put in a good word for me. From then on, as they say, the rest is history. I eventually became Director of Criminal Justice Planning for Fairfield County, Connecticut, because the Police Chiefs I worked for as part of the LEAA grant lobbied on my behalf.

When funding for the LEAA began to run out, I knew it was time to look for another job. I saw an ad in the *Wall Street Journal*. An organization in New York City was looking for someone with an MBA (which I didn't have) and/or a law degree (which I didn't have). There were several other requirements listed, none of which I had, so I knew the job was for me. I sent in my resume, and then made a pest of myself over the next few weeks by calling regularly to see if I could set up an appointment for an interview. I wouldn't take no for an answer and eventually wore them down. The position was Assistant to the Executive Director of the Association of Management Consulting Firms. When I was shown in to the Executive Director's office for the interview, he proceeded to let me know that I did not meet any of the requirements set out in the advertisement for the job, and the only reason he was meeting with me was because, like me, he was an ex-cop. It's not what you know, it's who you know. We traded war stories, both from our law enforcement background and from the military, and I got the job. I spent the next 17 years with ACME—the Association of Management Consulting Firms, eventually replacing the Executive Director when he retired and ultimately becoming President and Chief Executive Officer of the association.

As President and CEO of ACME, I ran an international organization. I had offices in New York City and in Brussels, Belgium. I met regularly with congressmen and senators and served as an advisor to several Eastern European countries as they broke away from the Soviet Union. I may not have had any of the educational or work-related experience that the association was looking for when they first hired me, but I brought something even more important with me—I had learned how to network.

In 1996 I decided to step down from my position at ACME to devote more time to speaking, consulting and writing. I became a professional member of the National Speakers Association and authored the book, *Insider's Guide to Consulting Success*. I now serve as consult to other consulting firms and to companies, governmental agencies, and not-for-profit organizations in the areas of strategy, marketing and mergers and acquisitions. My success in each of these endeavors can be traced back to one common source—networking, asking other people what I could do for them.

Now you have the secret to success in both personal and business relationships. It doesn't matter if you are a shy, bashful Mama's Boy or Girl or the life of the party. Networking is about wanting to help people who, in turn, want to help you. This book is designed to provide you with a methodology for getting the most out of your networks. In this book Frank and I will hopefully help you avoid some of the mistakes we made along the way, as well as give you the opportunity to learn from our successes. But this is not just our story. It is the story of those countless numbers of people who have helped us and who have been and are currently part of our networks. Any success we may have achieved has not been the result of what we know, but rather who we know and how we have learned to put the 7 Secrets of Successful Networking into practice.

PURPOSE AND OVERVIEW OF SUCCESSFUL BUSINESS NETWORKING

WHY DO YOU NEED THIS BOOK?

We designed this system for the sole purpose of helping people become more successful at their business now and over the long term. If you want to create greater profits for yourself and your business with a system that takes advantage of the principles successful businesspeople have been using for generations, this book will show you how to achieve that goal. This is not a get rich quick scheme. This system is the way to develop a long-term financially sound business.

The system we have developed in this book is setting the standard for more effective networking. In this book you will learn how this system will allow you to invest less time, energy and money, yet yield greater rewards.

WHO IS THIS BOOK FOR?

If you are:

- ○ an Independent Sales Representative who would like to increase your income with less "Sales" effort,

- ○ a Corporate Executive who wants to make sure your future is secure with your current company, another company or eventually your own business,

- ○ an Entrepreneur just starting up or an employee of a successful company and you want to reach greater financial success,

- ○ a Multi-Level-Marketing or Network Marketing Representative (Amway, LCI, NuSkin, TPN, Rexall, etc.) who wants to build an extensive down-line that will produce greater results,

- ○ a Student wanting to create a path of success for your future,

- ○ a Homemaker who wants to get into the work force in the future,

- ○ currently Unemployed and want to find a career in the area of your passion,

...then this book can show you how to achieve your goals. Networking is essential in every aspect of business.

PURPOSE AND OVERVIEW OF SUCCESSFUL BUSINESS

- If you are interested in having a team of people who can effectively create greater business for you than you can alone, this book will show you how to create that team.

- The system contained in this book is for people who are willing to dedicate themselves to growing their business and helping others to grow their business.

- This system is for unselfish people—those who believe in and live by the Golden Rule: Do unto others as you would have them do unto you.

- It is for people who understand that successful business means that each individual businessperson benefits when all businesses look out for each other.

What does this book contain?

The system developed in this book is found in the 7 Secrets, which are the fundamentals of every successful business:

1 Organization

2 Evaluation

3 Research & Development

4 Skills Development

5 Sales & Marketing

6 New Market Expansion

7 Maintenance

We will show you how Networking, Word-of-Mouth Marketing and Referrals are not the same thing, but are interdependent with one another. By Networking Effectively (building relationships) you will develop a Word-of-Mouth Marketing System (education/training/promotion) that will lead to Qualified Referrals (sales/potential sales).

Networking	Is	Relationship Building
⬇		⬇
Word-of-Mouth Marketing	Is	Education, Training
⬇		⬇
Referrals	Are	Sales, Potential Sales

How does this system work?

It shows you how to organize and operate your business more effectively. By organizing the people you know into your various networking levels, you will see that you already have an extensive network that you can easily build upon.

Once you are using the system, you can then encourage your Primary and Secondary Networkers to use the same system. They will then proactively try to help you as you are helping them, and they will be thankful to you for helping them become more successful at their business.

You can use the *Successful Business Networking* System for what we call the 4 Ms: Make Myself More Money. You do this by BOPB: Building Other People's Business.

As you will see, this is not about your running other people's businesses or working on theirs and ignoring your own. It is about finding out how you can help them and educating them as to how they can help you. If you help them by referring business to them then they will help you.

Is this some new scheme, system or marketing device that will be forgotten about in a year?

The idea of growing your business through Networking, Word-of-Mouth Marketing and Referrals is not new. In fact, it is how business first began. However, what has been lacking is a standardized system for all to use that would create greater results for each of us by working together.

This system is not for the "the glass is half empty" person. You must want to be a positive and helpful person. If you know the value of teamwork and enjoy the victory of others as well as your own, this system will work well for you. This system hasn't just been invented. It is what truly successful people have been doing for years.

Part I

GETTING STARTED

Chapter 1

NETWORKING WHYS AND WHEREFORES

A HALF-DOZEN REASONS TO NETWORK

While much of this book is devoted to helping you become a better networker by teaching you the secrets of how, what, where, when and who, we also want you to know *why* you should network.

To begin with, let's first look at some reasons for *not* networking. You don't need to network if:

○ you've already got all the business you can possibly handle for now, and you're not going to ever need new business in the future.

3

- you are the only person (or business) who does what you do, and everybody anywhere in the world who could possibly use your services already knows you.

- your social life is as full, rich and interesting as it can possibly be, and you will never want to meet another person.

- you're a confirmed and happy hermit living in a cave in Tibet (in which case you probably wouldn't be reading this book in the first place).

If you're still reading at this point, the above exclusions probably don't apply to you, so let's look at 6 reasons why you need to network:

1 To Build a Personal Sales Force

2 To Diversify Your Business

3 To Polish Your Sales Pitch

4 It's Important to Your Career

5 To Open a World of Possibilities

6 To Get Ahead of the Competition

1. **To Build a Personal Sales Force.** Networking provides you with a sales force for you and your business. By connecting with people and letting them know that you are interested in them and want to help them succeed, pretty soon they will want to know more about you and how they can be of assistance to you.

Let's face it, in today's competitive business place, you need all the help you can get. Having a group of people on your side helping you to market your business makes a lot more sense than trying to go it alone. And chances are, there are probably dozens of people who are already part of your network if you stop to think about it. Members of your family, people at your church or synagogue, the parents or friends of your children, your own friends, people you grew up with or went to school or college with, members of clubs or organizations you belong to, etc.—all are potential members of your personal sales force. By using the secrets you'll learn in this book, soon you will not only have more friends and acquaintances, but all of them will be engaging in a word-of-mouth marketing campaign on your behalf. And as any advertising or marketing expert can tell you, it is much more effective to have other people say good things about you or your products than to say them yourself. Why do you think major companies spend so much money to hire famous people to be their spokespersons? By applying a systematic and conscientious approach to networking, you can have your own spokespersons—and without spending any money to hire them.

2. **To Diversify Your Business**. There is strength in diversity. It is human nature for people to tend to associate with others with whom they have things in common. We tend to live in neighborhoods with others of a particular economic class. We worship with those of similar faith. We join clubs or organizations made up of people with business interests similar to our own, and so on. But in business, doing so means you're missing out on a huge market you may not even know about.

By conscientiously expanding your network, you can develop a sales force of different races, religions, genders and ethnicities—people who have different interests than you. What you do share, however, is a desire to help one another.

Rather than continuing to associate only with people just like yourself, look for and take advantage of opportunities to participate in activities, groups, organizations, clubs, etc., where you are likely to find the experts you need. Don't necessarily settle for ready-made groups. Customize your own networking group, and make it as diverse as possible.

Also, don't overlook the power of the Internet when putting your network together. You can be on-line and communicating instantly with people around the world whom you can help and who may be in a position to help you.

3. **To Polish Your Sales Pitch**. Networking provides you with an opportunity to practice your pitching. A network offers you a safe place to try out new sales approaches or marketing materials. It is helpful to know if you've got "good stuff" before you go out and start pitching for new business. Your network can tell you if your materials or approach work before you attempt to use it on that major prospective client or customer.

Ask the members of your network to listen to your presentation or to review your materials, and offer to do the same for them. The members of your network can let you know if your planned approach is clear and likely to be effective or if you need to spend more time in the bullpen warming up.

Develop a new line to use on that special someone you'd like to meet. Develop arguments to use on your boss when asking for a raise. Respond to questions and answers in a job interview. Develop a presentation or plan a speech. Whatever you need to do, you can use your network as a sounding board to have them tell you if you're on the right track. Your network can help you avoid mistakes and keep you from making a fool of yourself.

NETWORKING WHYS AND WHEREFORES

Engaging in role playing with members of your network is also a very effective practice. You'll get to see how other people perform and respond in situations similar to those which you will be facing. Learning tips and techniques that have made other members of your network successful can help you improve your own chances of succeeding.

4. **It's Important to Your Career**. Networks are important at all stages of your career. Successful networking depends on the kinetic energy of people helping people. It is not static or inanimate, and it is as helpful when you are first starting out in your career as it can be in helping you keep your balance atop the pinnacle of your profession.

One of the biggest mistakes people just starting out in business make is being afraid to ask for help. By and large, most successful people are flattered when someone asks for their advice or opinion. Finding the right people to ask is not as hard as you might think.

Chances are you already know (or perhaps at least your parents may know) some older people who are experienced in business. It is quite likely that these people, in turn, have a wide range of contacts. The networks that your family friends have developed over the years can be put to work for you and many times are yours simply for the asking. Make an appointment to visit with your family's attorney or tax accountant—or maybe you've got a wealthy relative whom you can approach. Maybe your parents could arrange for you to meet with their bosses. The objective of getting together with them is not to ask for a job, but just to receive a little friendly advice concerning your career. We'd be willing to bet that at least some, if not all, of these people would be willing to help you. And once they have decided to help you, they are committed to helping you succeed. After all, they don't want to look bad in front of members of their networks to whom they will introduce you.

Hook onto as many mentors, guides, counselors and coaches as you can, and never be too proud to ride their coattails as high as they can take you.

5. **To Open a World of Possibilities**. Networking gives you a world of possibilities. In years gone by, most people's networks were by-and-large confined to a fairly narrow geographic area, but in today's world of e-mail, faxes and worldwide overnight delivery services, it is practically as easy and inexpensive to develop a global network as it is to keep in touch locally.

All it takes to begin to develop a global network is to ask the members of your present network if they do much traveling. There is always someone here who has been there and who knows someone you should meet. Explore opportunities to identify both social and business contacts in different countries of the world. Bankers, students and faculty members at your local college, and employees of international companies are all good places to begin your investigation.

Regardless of the natural beauty or historic edifices in any country around the world, there is always a feeling of being disconnected or alone when you visit a foreign country and don't know a soul. If you use your network properly, you'll be able to go anywhere and everywhere and have someone to help you appreciate the real culture of the country and to find new business opportunities or resources.

6. **To Get Ahead of the Competition**. Stay one step ahead of the competition. There is no truth to the rumor that you can succeed in business without really trying. You have to know what your competitors are up to, and then find ways to stay ahead of them. This is what your network can help you do.

NETWORKING WHYS AND WHEREFORES

The government spends billions of dollars each year on what used to be called spying, but is now known by the more genteel name of "intelligence gathering." Various agencies have thousands of people trying to learn the secrets of both friends and foes. While we are not advocating that you turn your network into secret agents, it does pay to keep in mind that people love to talk. Former employees of your competitors, particularly if they are upset over factors which contributed to their being referred to as "former," are always searching for a sympathetic ear willing to listen to their tales of woe. The information they are willing to provide about your competitors can help you keep track of such things as who they are hiring and what skill sets they are seeking. Are they having trouble with any of their customers? Are they getting ready to introduce new products and services? Is a new advertising campaign about to break? If they are your competitors, you can't afford to be the last to know. It is always important to have a pipeline into your competition. Keep your eyes and ears open, and ask the members of your network to do the same and share advance knowledge about what your competition is up to.

More than 50 percent of all businesses go out of business within their first seven years of existence. If you don't want to add to that statistic, you need to have an edge over your competition. If you are offering the same products or services to the same customers using the same marketing techniques as your competitors, you are going to be hard pressed to gain a competitive edge. You can't control the economy, and you can't control your competitors, but you can control your response to the economy and to your competitors. Your network can serve as an "advance warning system" of both economic and competitive changes, thereby providing you with an opportunity to respond proactively.

Networking also helps you gain a competitive advantage in other ways. The old adage, "Build a better mousetrap, and the world will beat a path to your door," works only if the world knows about your mousetrap.

FIVE WAYS TO MARKET YOUR BUSINESS

In reality, there are five ways to market your business:

1 **You can advertise**. It doesn't matter if you place your ads on television, radio, billboards, or even matchbook covers—it's still advertising. And it can be very effective.

   But advertising is also very expensive. You have to choose your options and opportunities carefully. It is also hard to measure the effectiveness of advertising. Competition for attention from your customers is huge. It is estimated that people are subjected to almost 2,000 advertising messages every day. They are inundated by products and services which after a while all begin to sound and look alike. You can't afford not to advertise at all however, because all of your competitors do so. But since you probably don't have an unlimited budget or an inexhaustible supply of creativity, advertising alone is not the answer.

2 **You can undertake a public relations (PR) campaign**. Properly managed and funded, PR can be very effective in enhancing your firm's name recognition and reputation. But it can also be very expensive and time consuming, especially for small companies. It is also important to understand that public relations may be able to lay the groundwork for getting new business,

NETWORKING WHYS AND WHEREFORES

but it does not close the sale. Its effectiveness can rarely be felt on your bottom line over a short period of time.

3 **You can engage in that dreaded activity known as cold calling.** The very idea of going out and banging on doors brings back painful memories of long ago high school days going from door to door selling magazine subscriptions to try to earn some extra spending money. A properly managed and motivated sales force can undoubtedly sell your products and services to at least a percentage of the establishments on whose doors they knock, but cold calling, whether in person or through telemarketers, is expensive and time consuming. It also results in a high degree of turnover among your salespeople. After all, most human beings can only accept so much rejection before they burn out.

4 **You can participate in trade shows.** Setting up a display of your products and services at a location where your prospective customers are likely to be gathered can be a viable marketing resource.

Trade shows also offer the additional benefit of providing you with an opportunity to see what your competitors have to offer. By walking around the halls of the exhibition, you can get an idea of what new products and services are entering the market, and you will be able to see which of your customers are spending time with your competitors. But again, especially for small companies, participating in trade shows can be an expensive undertaking. Not only is there the cost of purchasing or renting the exhibit itself, but you also have to pay for the right to be in the trade show. Add to this the cost of shipping, setting up and dismantling, meals, hotel rooms, transportation, etc., and suddenly the bills add up, and the cost becomes quite large.

5 The most cost-effective marketing activity is to increase your business through **word of mouth.** This is where your network comes in.

NOTE

Developing and using a network of contacts in an organized and systematic way can provide you with a worldwide sales force without the associated payroll costs.

A name on a business card or in your address file is not a network. Just as you would not pour money into an advertising or public relations campaign, or sign up to participate in a trade show or send your salespeople out on sales calls without a plan, so too effective word-of-mouth marketing through referrals provided by your network requires a fine-tuned approach. This book gives you the secrets to making networking really work. Read on, and learn from the pros.

Chapter 2

WHAT IS NETWORKING?

DOING WHAT COMES NATURALLY

Your networking first started when you looked up at your parents and laughed, cried or acknowledged them for the first time. A new relationship was born. Relationship building is synonymous with networking. If you have always been one of those people who gets along with everyone, makes friends easily and can fit in with any crowd, you already have the foundation for being a strong, effective and successful networker. If you feel that your abilities in these areas have been lacking, then you have to develop better communication and networking skills. Fortunately, that's what this book is all about.

Your networking consciously started when you first needed or wanted something and asked someone you knew to help you get it. When you wanted your first bicycle, you asked your parents for one. They, in turn, asked a friend to recommend a bicycle shop or if they knew of someone selling a used bicycle. Their friends may have recommended a bicycle shop and told what bike they purchased, what a good deal they got on it and how nice the salesperson was, and that they knew they could go back to the shop anytime if they had any problems or questions to be answered. Or maybe they referred your parent to some neighbors to purchase a used bicycle from friends. They were happy to buy a bicycle from friends because they knew them to be honest and to give a good deal. Both of the above scenarios are examples of networking.

However, business networking is very different from personal networking. Although the principles of networking hold true, there are specific skills in business networking that must be developed. In many ways it is similar to playing a sport. In order to become proficient at any sport there are certain principles of training that must be followed: discipline, focus, consistency, perseverance and practice. Although for each sport specific skills and drills will vary, these principles will hold. The same is true in networking. The fundamental skills you have developed in personal networking have given you a good base, but they have not prepared you for the big leagues of business networking.

BUSINESS NETWORKING

So that we all have the same understanding of the term, let's define **Business Networking**. Network is made up of two words: Net and

Work. Your "Net" is made up of the people you interconnect with in business. Like a net that catches fish, all these people and businesses are interconnected, if by no other commonality than yourself. It is this interconnectedness that creates the greater power, efficiency and ability for you to capture business. If you have a weak connection in the net, you will dramatically decrease its effectiveness. Your "Work" is the actual building and maintenance of that net. You are responsible for building this net larger and stronger on a daily basis. You must also keep up on its maintenance so it remains strong. If there are weak connections, you must strengthen or replace them. Otherwise, you may let that "big fish" escape.

As you build your network, you will want to be selective about whom you allow to be part of it. You want to build a quality network that you know you can rely on. As you grow, your network can change and improve with you. You never want to lose contact with your original **Primary Networkers**, but through the natural cycle of business relations they will rotate through your different **Networking Categories**.

NETWORKING IS MARKETING

Being an Effective Networker means that you are making sales because your marketing strategy is causing, or "effecting," the sale. Some people have reputations as "Great" Networkers, yet they are not increasing their business. Your goal should be to be an Effective Networker not a Great Networker. A "Great Networker" is a person that everyone knows, yet no one is buying from. You know who I mean, that guy who passes out business cards to everyone but builds relationships with no one. An Effective Networker creates a successful business by making the sale while maintaining their integrity and ethics. The Effective Networker may not be known by everyone but the people they are known to are doing business with them, not just talking about them. They are creating a quality network that will provide them with qualified information, contacts, connections and referrals.

Remember that marketing your "self" is primary and that marketing your "business" is secondary. If this is the opposite of what you have done in the past, then this skill alone will make a difference in your Effective Networking. People don't network or build relationships with a business, they network with people. When I refer one of the people in my network, I am referring my trust, confidence and relationship to them. They just happen to be in the business that someone I know is looking for.

We've all known people who have changed careers. Did changing careers deter you from referring that person to a business? More than likely, not. You have a relationship with that person and their abilities. No matter what business they go into, you know they will use the same principles of business as before; they are just changing their skills. Marketing yourself starts with communication skills (verbal and non-verbal), knowledge of your profession and the desire or passion you have for your work. These three factors will convey your professional image. The confidence you build in your Networking Associates about yourself comes from how they perceive you. Creating the correct image is one of the primary skills of marketing.

For example, let's say I am a financial planner, and I'm meeting with you about becoming part of my network.

Scenario 1: The first time we are to meet I pick you up in my brand new Mercedes. I am wearing an expensive suit with a silk designer tie. I walk right up to you, stick out my hand, introduce myself and tell you

WHAT IS NETWORKING?   17

how pleased I am to meet you and how I've been looking forward to this lunch to see how I can send some business your way. What is your perception of me? Professional, successful, sincere in purpose.

Scenario 2: I pick you up in my 10-year-old Hyundai Excel. I have on a pair of jeans and a button-down oxford. I wave you into the car, say hello after you get in and ask you where you want to go for our meeting. What is your perception of me? Not very successful, casual, new in business, not sure of what his purpose is.

The two examples above show how your personal image is marketing you. You have to decide how you want to be perceived by your associates and then design your personal marketing plan to best achieve that. If the image you portray is different from the one you want, then your personal marketing strategy is not working. Remember, marketing is the process to achieve your goal. Your goal is to build a powerful network of associates who want to refer business to you and who will remember you when the opportunity arises. Marketing yourself means educating me on your various "features" and "benefits." The more educated I am, the easier it will be for me to remember you when I find someone who needs your product or service.

Do you remember Sales & Marketing 101? A feature is technical, a benefit is emotional.

NOTE

Feature: This car has a crushed leather interior.

Benefit: The rich crushed-leather interior provides a comfortable, quiet and safe ride so you can travel with total pleasure.

Are you interested in buying this car because of its crushed-leather interior or because of the pleasure you will receive from riding in it? Features attract, benefits sell. Your Networking Associates need to know your features and sell your benefits. Get them emotionally involved in who you are. Create a "want to help" attitude.

When marketing your business, you need to be specific about your message. Your associates need to know the different aspects of your business and what it is that you want. We all want the referral that is a potential sale, but you may also be looking for information, contacts or connections in terms of vendors, suppliers, associations, etc. As your Networking Associate, I need to understand what a good referral is for you and how to recognize the opportunity when it arises. I need to know what you do, when you do it, where you do it, how you do it, what makes you unique and why you are so good at it.

LET'S GET PHYSICAL

There is such a thing as low-, medium-, and high-tech networking (which will be discussed later) like the Internet, video conferencing, inter-office networks, broadcast faxes and e-mail. However, for most of us networking is a face-to-face activity. With the advent of cell phones, pagers, voice mail, faxes, home computers and affordable home copy machines, the less we need or have the opportunity to get out and meet with people. This technology may be great for our efficiency and productivity, but it hurts our daily interactive networking.

Effective Networking means you must get up, get out and get hand-to-hand, arm-to-arm and shoulder-to-shoulder with people. Before I

WHAT IS NETWORKING?

refer you a client, associate, friend or family member, I need to build confidence and trust in you. By meeting with you face-to-face, I can build a relationship with you quicker. Have you ever had a date over the phone? You may have started it over the phone, but you dated in person. This allows for a much more personal and bonding relationship. Business is the same. Do people refer business to others by building relationships over the phone? It happens, but not very often. It is an out-of-sight, out-of-mind scenario. There is no loyalty in a high-tech relationship. People need to look each other in the eye and have open, honest communication in order to build long-lasting, effective business relationships.

When I meet with you one-on-one, I have committed time to the relationship. If I have a phone relationship with you, ending our relationship is as easy as hanging up the phone or not taking or returning your phone calls. When I meet with you in person, I have a physical, mental and emotional commitment to you. It's much harder for me to discard a relationship with a person versus a voice on the phone.

When you go car shopping, the best thing for that salesman to do is sit you down and start the negotiating process with you as soon as possible. When you start negotiating price with him, whether or not you are ready to buy, you are investing in that relationship. You are committing time and energy in creating a relationship with that salesperson. When you are ready to buy, you will more than likely go back to that salesperson because of the investment you have made. If you go to a new dealership, you will have to recreate a new relationship with a new person, and that takes more time and energy. The emotional commitment you have with the current salesperson, good or bad, is stronger than the one you don't have at all. Networking is the same. The more time we spend together discussing business and other things, the more of a commitment we invest in our relationship. Getting physical with your networkers is one of the skills of Effective Networking.

SOMETIMES BAD THINGS HAPPEN TO GOOD PEOPLE

Do you remember that client who was unhappy with the product or service you provided them, and no matter what you tried to do to help resolve the problem, they left dissatisfied? We've all had them. Did you know that, on average, one person told 13 others of the bad experience with you? And those 13 probably each told another three or four. On the other end of the spectrum, a happy client who leaves your business on Cloud Nine tells only four others of their pleasant experience with you. This doesn't seem quite fair. According to these statistics, you have to fully satisfy 52 clients for every one you don't satisfy.

What you need to do is to create a network of people who can battle these fires for you. The larger the network of associates who believe in you, the greater your firefighting team. You have to become proactive, not reactive, in the word-of-mouth marketing of your business. If you wait for something bad to happen before you do something to battle it, it's too late.

In the old West when a building was on fire, people would react by lining up and grabbing buckets, filling them up at the well, and passing them down until they were thrown on the fire. A noble effort, but very ineffective. No building was ever saved because they were reacting, and it was too late. Today we have firehouses with trucks and professionals trained to fight fires. The technology we make use of today to fight fires is a proactive way of stopping the tragedy. We have a system in place to take care of the problem instantly, as it arises.

Building your network is the same. If you don't have a network out there, by the time you hear about the bad word-of-mouth circulating, the damage has been done. You can't really do much about it. However, by actively developing your network, your associates can put out the fire before it grows and becomes unmanageable. Your associates' opinions mean a lot to people because they are seen as objective third parties and have no direct relationship to your business, so their defense of you is meaningful.

Chapter 3

YOU CAN'T AFFORD NOT TO NETWORK

TIME IS YOUR MOST PRECIOUS COMMODITY—TRADE IT WELL

"I'm too busy for networking. These mixers, socials, breakfasts, luncheons and cocktail parties are just a waste of time. Nobody does business at them." If you have thoughts even similar to this, then you have a lot to learn about networking. Keep in mind that business socials are not meant for business. They are meant to be social events. They are chances for you to get to know your business associates better and for them to get to know you. This relationship building is a key to long-term business networking effectiveness.

One of my associates, Bob, who lives in the next town, has a computer training and consulting business. When he first got involved in business networking he wasn't a real believer in it. I told him that he had to get together one-on-one with the key people he knew so they could learn more about him. He hemmed and hawed about it, but he finally changed his schedule and started taking one appointment out for lunch each week to start networking. In the last year he has made about $14,000 just from referrals from those people. You have to understand, this money came while he was sitting in his office working on some other job. His phone rang, and people told him they wanted to hire him because he came so highly recommended by their friend, associate, client, etc. He told me just the other day that an accountant he's been getting together with for the last year just referred him a computer job for a dentist's office which is $30,000 worth of business for him. Guess who believes in networking now? What did it cost him? Time and maybe a few lunches. Not a bad way to make a living. I love it when people call and say they want to hire me before we have even met. I could get used to that. Networking does take time, but think of all the enjoyable networking activities available to you: golf, tennis, sailing, yachting, hiking, softball, bowling, fishing, skiing, eating, wine tasting... need I go on? Networking comes in all shapes and sizes. It could be an association meeting of your profession or a professional basketball game with a potential client. Be creative, take time, have fun. Remember, everyone wants to do business with people they know, like and trust. With time invested, that could be you, every time.

CLIMBING THE NET OF SUCCESS...
NO LADDERS NEEDED

A new job may be in the company or industry you've always dreamed of or the next step up in your current place of employment. If you develop a strong network, your Net will be your ladder to success. Developing strong relationships with key people is the "in" you need to get your career off and running. Who are "key people"? You never know.

When someone is put in charge of hiring another, their reputation is on the line and, possibly, their job. The person they hire has to be an asset to the company, not a liability. They need to know that the person they hire is knowledgeable, professional, reliable, trustworthy and will produce for the company.

If it were you doing the hiring, out of the following five choices, rate the way you would like to make a decision to hire someone.

1 A friend says their brother does that job somewhere else, and they'll have him call you.

2 A person answers an ad you ran in the paper.

3 A coworker says they know someone who would be perfect for the job.

4 A person in-house says they would like the position.

5 You think a business associate you know from the local Chamber of Commerce would be perfect.

All of the above job applicants have come to you through networking, except the person who answered the ad in the paper. You don't want to prejudge this person; however, the advantage all the others have is that they already have a person to vouch for them. Instead of calling blind references, you have a referral from someone who is already in your network. Doesn't that make you feel a little more comfortable in your decision?

This is one of many ways the power of a good network can benefit you now and in the future. If you are looking for a job, at the present time or not, developing a strong network can allow you to catch that perfect career in your net.

NEED IT, WANT IT, WANT TO BUY OR SELL IT. . .

A car, a bicycle, sports equipment, tools, golf clubs, real estate, consulting advice and whatever else you can think of can be acquired through your network of associates. In business, one of the most valuable things you can acquire from your networking associates is information.

If within your network you have others who are in the same profession as you, professions that compliment your own and professions that are your potential clients, you have a powerful resource of information.

Let's say you are a salesperson for a large corporation. You receive an appointment with a representative from a profession you have never done business with before. This could be a major account for you and could open many doors in the future. Your presentation must really impress them and show that you really understand their needs. What would be the best way to prepare for the presentation? Wouldn't it be great if you had an inside person at the company who could tell you what they really want? Since you don't have that, what about the next best thing? A person who is in the same profession but works for

YOU CAN'T AFFORD NOT TO NETWORK

a different company. If you have a strong and diversified network, you may have that perfect person at your beck and call. Or if you have strategically aligned yourself with other associates that do what you do, they could tell you of their experience with another company in the same profession as your potential client.

You may need to buy the right gift for a client, your significant other or your child. How do you find that right gift? You want quality at a good price. You need to know you are not getting ripped off on the price and that if there are any problems, you will have no trouble getting satisfaction from your place of purchase. You don't want to buy a diamond engagement ring or an expensive watch from the vendor on the corner. Your networks can save you time and money far in excess of the effort you put into building them.

Part II

ORGANIZATION

SECRET 1:

THERE ARE 5 NETWORKER CATEGORIES

Chapter 4

TAKING INVENTORY

NETWORKING GOALS

Where do you want to be in five, 10, 15 years? To make your networking effective, you must have specific goals. The more specific you make your goals in life, the more likely you are to achieve them. Once you have focused on your long-term goals and set up your short-term goals to get there, you can use networking to help you achieve them.

One of the best ways to do this is to start by "modeling." To model another means to try to recreate what they did to reach their level of success. If you can recreate it for yourself, then your likelihood of success will increase dramatically.

Here are some questions you must answer to see what it will take for you to achieve what your models have:

1 Where did they start from, socio-economically?

2 Who did their parents know?

3 What is their educational background?

4 What is their professional background?

5 What groups and organizations have they belonged to?

6 What is the difference between what they had to start and what you have now?

7 How can you make similar connections to similar groups as they did?

8 Who do you know right now that can directly help you make some contacts?

9 Who do you know who might know someone who can help you? Will they?

10 Who do you want to know?

11 What circles do you want to be in?

12 How can you help the people you need to help you?

The questions above will help you take an inventory of where you are at now in contrast to where you are trying to get to. It is important to be completely honest with yourself. Once you know exactly what you need to do to network yourself to the next level, you can set your networking plan in motion.

TAKING INVENTORY

After you have answered all the questions above, you must have the right mindset before you go forward. Before you meet one person or go to one meeting or event to network yourself, you must think, "How can I help the people in my network?" "What can I do for them?"

Never try to sell yourself to your networking associates until they are ready to help you. The key is to always do something for them first, with honesty, sincerity and conviction. You are trying to build a long-lasting relationship with these people, not use them to get what you want. The relationship is where all the long-term benefits will come.

Let's say we have just recently met, and you would like me to introduce you to someone I know. If I feel you are simply using me and my connections for your own benefit, I may introduce you to my friend or associate, but later on when they speak with me one-on-one about you, I will not give you praise. I may say to them, "He's a user," or "I don't trust him," or "I can't tell you anything good or bad, I don't know him well enough." None of these comments will be beneficial. Even though the last one seems non-committal, not committing to say something good about you is pretty negative. Remember, networking is about relationship building, not about using other people.

Are you thinking, "What can I give to those people I want in my network?" If nothing else, you can at least offer a true business friendship. Be a person that will try to get them some business or make connections for them, someone who is out there defending them and spreading good words about them. If someone you meet feels you are honest and sincere, they appreciate that; if you can get them some business, even better. We all have something we can give to another. You never know what that might be until you sit down with that person one-on-one and really get to know them. The key to success in networking is having the right mindset, that is, what can I *give*, not what can I *get*.

YOU KNOW MORE PEOPLE THAN YOU KNOW

We cannot emphasize strongly enough how important these next steps are to your networking system. If you follow these next steps, you will have organized the network of people you know so you can easily refer to them at any time, and you will be able to develop a system to increase your networking power. Although this may take a little time to do, *take the time to organize your networks*. Every time we do this with our consulting clients, we get the same reaction. People can't believe how many people they know, and in so many different professions.

One of the things you must do is find out how many contacts you really do have and what the quality of those contacts are. To do this, break down who you know into the 5 Networking Categories:

1 Primary

2 Secondary

3 Dormant

4 Inactive

5 Mailing List

Everyone you know, you have met or received a business card or a sales letter from can be categorized in your network. Why is it necessary that you do this? Because you have connections out there you don't even know about. By organizing your networks, you will learn who you know, what they do, what your current relationship is with them and how you can improve your relationship with them if you choose to. To be an effective networker, organization is the key. It may take a little time to get it all set up, but it will make your business and life much easier and more profitable.

Each person in your network, as you develop your relationship with them, will move up your networking steps toward your Primary Network. This is important because there are 3 different levels of referrals you will get from your networking associates: Simple, Compound and Complex—which we will discuss in greater detail later in this book.

YOUR FIVE NETWORKER CATEGORIES

1. **Primary**—these are the people who you are closest to and with whom you have contact on a daily and/or weekly basis. Your family, co-workers, best clients and friends are the people you have the closest relationships with. These are the people that you can call and ask for a favor, and they will do it for you. It is the people in this level of your network that you will develop a very strong referral-based relationship with. You would have no problem recommending them, and they have full confidence in recommending you. You might even have a mutually exclusive relationship with each other's business. You are never out of contact with each other for more than six weeks at any one time.

A friend of mine is a consultant. Whenever he sits down with a client and the client needs some new graphic design work, he brings in a woman who owns a graphic design studio for the job. He knows her work, her dependability and professionalism. She is now on the forefront of his Primary Network, and they refer each other a lot of business. He told me he used to call her just when he needed an estimate on a job or for her to see a client. Once he developed his Networking System, he made sure he was in contact with her at least every six weeks. Even if he didn't have work for her, she knew he was thinking of her and would give him priority whenever he or his clients needed her, and likewise, he would be fresh in her mind when she came across someone who could use his services. Since he made her part of his Primary Network, they both have increased their business.

2. **Secondary**—these are the people with whom you have contact on a regular basis. You speak with them every two to six months. They are no less valuable to you than the primary; they are just contacted by you less often. However, there will be a wide range of Secondary Networker relationships. Some may be in that every two months group, and others at that six-month period. If they are in your Secondary Network, they know you well and feel comfortable referring you, but they aren't quite ready to take the risk of going the extra mile for you by laying their reputation on the line with their best client, associate, or family member. They are not willing to do favors for you yet by calling on people in their own network to go to bat for you.

3. **Dormant**—your dormant networkers are those people you are in contact with every six to 12 months. This may be an old client, a college buddy, a non-immediate family member. As you go through your list of contacts, these are those people you've been meaning to keep in touch with on a more regular basis, but just haven't found the time. Even though you are not in contact with these people as frequently as you'd like, it's still likely that you could get referrals from them, just not as often.

4. **Inactive**—these are the people you haven't been in contact with in over a year. They are definitely inactive because you have pretty much forgotten about each other. Obviously the referrals you get from this group will be few and far between.

TAKING INVENTORY 37

5. **Mailing List**—this is pretty much your "other" list. These are people who you received a business card from, a brochure from or haven't spoken with in over two years. They are pretty much on your mailing list but not active in any way of referring business to you.

Obviously the ideal situation is to have everyone you know in your Primary Network; however, this is also unrealistic. There is a process to follow that will allow you to consistently move your networkers up to the next level in your network and enable them to find better quality referrals for you. The first thing you must do is put the defined networks above into action. So let's now take the time to really set up our system.

WRITE 'EM DOWN

First, let's put together your networks. If you have a computer and feel comfortable developing your own database, that would be ideal. If not, take out five pieces of paper. At the top right corner label them "Primary Network," "Secondary Network," "Dormant Network," "Inactive Network" and "Mailing List." Now divide each paper into four columns as shown on the following pages:

Name (last, first)

Phone (W for work, H for home)

Profession

Address

PRIMARY NETWORK

NAME: LAST, FIRST	PHONE	PROFESSION	ADDRESS

TAKING INVENTORY

SECONDARY NETWORK

NAME: LAST, FIRST	PHONE	PROFESSION	ADDRESS

DORMANT NETWORK

NAME: LAST, FIRST	PHONE	PROFESSION	ADDRESS

TAKING INVENTORY

INACTIVE NETWORK

NAME: LAST, FIRST	PHONE	PROFESSION	ADDRESS

SUCCESSFUL BUSINESS NETWORKING

MAILING LIST NETWORK

NAME: LAST, FIRST	PHONE	PROFESSION	ADDRESS

TAKING INVENTORY 43

Lay your five sheets in front of you. Start with your Primary Network Sheet, and put down the name of every person you feel qualifies as part of your Primary Network. Start with family, then friends, working associates, regular clients, vendors, etc. For the "Profession," if they do not work full time, put down their relationship to you, i.e. Friend, Family.

As you put down names in your Primary Network, if you come across people you don't feel fall into this category, then put their names in the categories you deem appropriate. Go through your address book, business card file, and wherever else you can think of to get names. When you come across a person and you're not sure where to categorize them, "should I put him in the secondary or dormant group?" always choose the lower group. This should motivate you to contact that person and move them up a level.

After you finish putting all the names of everyone you know—and we do mean everyone—you should have a good idea of where your networks stand. Later, in Chapter 14, we will discuss how to move people up in your network.

On the following page is a diagram of the average distribution of most people's networks. Are you above average or below? If below, you have some work to do. If above, then you have some pretty good networking skills already, so it should be pretty easy to consistently build your levels.

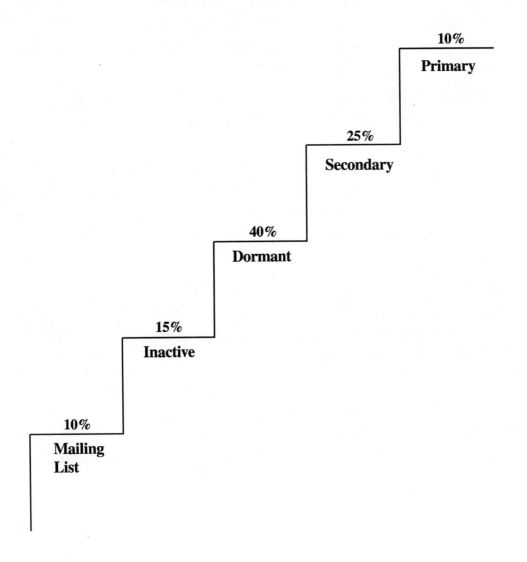

Average Distribution of People's Networks

MAKE SURE YOU'VE BEEN HONEST

Before moving on, go back through your networking categories and make sure you have been honest with yourself in terms of who is in what level. Sometimes we put people in a higher level because it just makes us feel better to pretend we have stronger connections with our networkers. It is important that you are honest and if anything, a little hard on yourself. It never hurts to put someone who is on the border of two categories into the lower one. This keeps you in check. By putting your associates falsely into the upper category, you may develop a false sense of security with these people. You will think you are closer to them than you actually are. When you don't get the results from them that you expect, you will be disappointed, and this will create bad feelings between yourself and your Networking Associate.

NOTE

If you have not done the above steps, please stop now and sit down and organize your networks. Getting yourself well organized in this system is what will make you more efficient and successful. If you have organized everyone you know into your 5 networker categories, congratulations! You are ready to organize your time in the same efficient manner. The next section will show you how to use your time more effectively.

Chapter 5

NETWORKER'S DAILY ORGANIZER

ORGANIZING AND OPERATING EFFECTIVELY

Most business professionals have some type of Daily Organizer. We, the authors, have tried every organizer we could find over the last 10 to 15 years. Even though we thought they all were good and had their unique advantages, neither of us could ever stick with them. They all seemed too restrictive and had too much stuff we didn't need and not enough of what would have been helpful. Being very entrepreneurial, we both have been involved in various business ventures and projects, and we also have personal and family responsibilities. As entrepreneurs we needed to organize many things at once, as well as have an efficient way to organize our networks, appointments and sales calls. We decided to come up with our own system that would be easy to use and effective in every aspect of our lives. What we designed is a way for you to organize yourself so you can keep track of the different responsibilities you have in your life. For instance, besides being a business professional, you may also be a spouse, parent, coach, mentor, volunteer, association officer, weekend athlete, and so on. Having these different aspects to your life, each with its own and sometimes overlapping networks, you need to keep track of the many different roles you have at the same time. This organizational system will allow you to do that.

Organization is the first step to any responsibility you take on. If you are not organized, you are going to waste valuable time. Time, in business, is money. It is almost impossible to be over-organized, although there seem to be some people who spend all their time organizing and none of it actually doing anything. That is why it is important that your organizational system works hand in hand with your operational system. It's nice to be able to see all the things you have to do and when you have to do them, but it is meaningless if you don't have a plan for achieving them. By adopting this **Organizational and Operational System**, you can become more effective at everything you do. Effectiveness is accomplishing what you need to, when you need to, successfully. How nice would it be for you to get everything done that you wanted to, on time, correctly and then have time to sit and enjoy the fruits of your labor? Read on!

NETWORKER'S DAILY ORGANIZER

NOTE

All of the following sections are designed and written so you can produce each of these charts on your computer and print them out. This also allows you to customize each section to your specific needs. All the forms used in this Chapter were produced by us on a home computer in the Microsoft Publisher '97 program. If you don't have a publishing program, you could do this in most word processing programs, but it will take a little more time.

There are a few other options:

○ You could buy the computer disk from us with all the forms on it, ready for you to customize and print out. Call our publisher. The telephone number is in the front of this book.

○ You could copy the documents we have here for your personal use. They would have to be enlarged or reduced, depending on the size of your organizer.

○ You could call the publisher directly and order the sheets we have here. The number is in the front of the book.

○ You could buy the "Successful Business Networking" complete daily organizer system. This is also available through our publisher.

Here are the different sections we will be designing:

1 Networking Associates Address Book

2 Prioritized "To Do" List

3 Responsibility Note Pads

4 "Real Life" Appointment Schedule

5 Short- & Long-Term Goals, Master Sheet

6 Calendar Choices

NETWORKING ASSOCIATES ADDRESS BOOK

You probably have some type of address book in your organizer. The problem with most of these is that they are not very efficient or user friendly in terms of having your more frequently contacted networkers handy and the least contacted ones somewhere else. We know that it's unlikely you can put all the people you know into your address book. However, because you have just organized everyone you know into your 5 Networker Categories, you can prioritize who you will have in your address book.

The first group of Networking Associates you know you want in it are those in your Primary Network. The next group is your Secondary Networkers, the third your Dormant Networkers. If you find you have been able to fit these three groups in without a problem, then you can go on to your Inactive and Mailing List Networks. This prioritizing that you have already done in Chapter 4 makes organizing your Address Book quite easy. If names have to be left out, you start with your Mailing List and work your way up the categories. However, you should keep as many sections with you as possible. You never know how you may be able to help someone by connecting them with one of your distant, lower level networkers. Once you do refer a Networking Associate from one of your lower levels, you have given yourself the opportunity to reestablish a relationship with that person and move them up to a higher networking category. This is the beauty of a well organized system.

A while back I was having lunch with a Networking Associate of mine, and he mentioned he wanted to do a direct mail piece to the homes in the county surrounding his business. He asked if I could recommend someone. I thought for a moment and then looked in the Inactive Networker section of my organizer. I found the name of a guy I had done business with a few years earlier. I hadn't used him or spoken to him in years, but I knew that he was still in business. I gave my friend his name and told him that when I last worked with him, things went great. I said I would give my direct mail associate a phone call and have him contact my inquiring friend. When I returned to my office after lunch, I called my direct mail associate and reintroduced myself to him. He said he remembered me, and we caught up for a moment. I then told him that I had just given his name out and that he should call this friend of mine. He was extremely appreciative. I then asked if we could have lunch in the next week so I could find out more about his business and see if I could send him any more business. What do you think he said? He was excited and is now part of my Primary Network. Being organized allows you to operate so you never miss the opportunity to help someone and thereby build your network. I was able to help two people fulfill their needs, and I got another person out there plugging for me. Gotta love it!

The objective is not to just have your associates' names, addresses and phone numbers, but to have all the information necessary for you to refer them out to prospective customers when you find the opportunity.

The five separate Address Book sections will all use the same format so let's start with your Primary Networkers.

If you have the Microsoft Publisher '97 program in your computer, then go to the blank page screen and click on the table icon on the left side of the screen; drag it to full page.

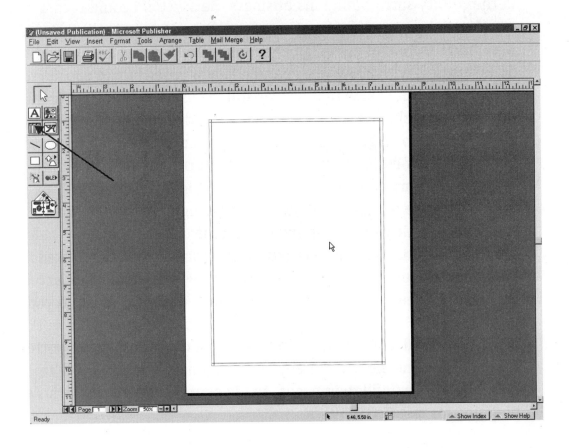

NETWORKER'S DAILY ORGANIZER

When the "Create Table" box comes up, choose 24 Rows and 5 Columns.

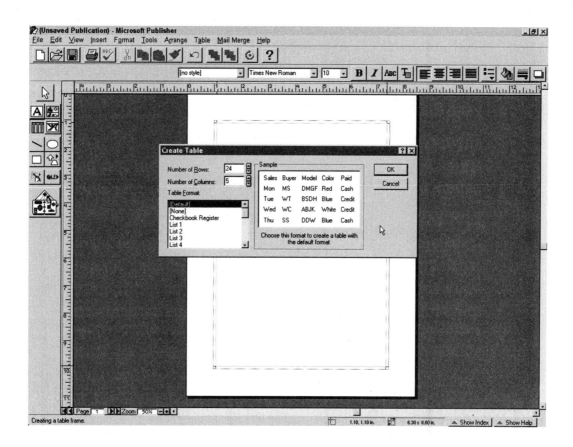

Then, from the "Table Format" box, choose "Numbers 5."

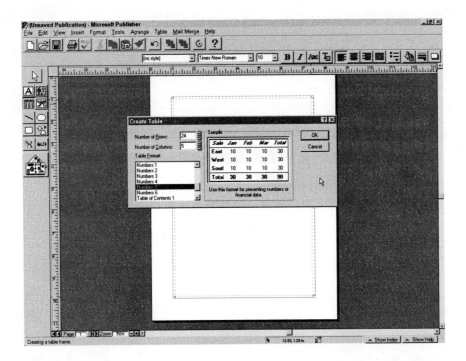

If you do not have this software program, then you need to find which program in your computer can produce "Tables." Once you have found that, then customize the table to 24 rows with 5 columns. We have found that once we have the tables set up, we want to make them a little bigger. This is not problem. You can expand the size of the table at any time by clicking on the table and adjusting one of the resize handles.

NETWORKER'S DAILY ORGANIZER

We have the Networker information broken down into 15 sections. The list below gives the name of each section from left to right and top to bottom, respectively.

1. **Name**: **Last, First**—arranged by last name, alphabetically, for easy reference.

> Name: Last, First
> Johnson, Nina

2. **Profession**—categorized by profession. Your own system may not necessarily have exact professional categories. For instance, instead of putting "Optometrist," you might want to put, "Doctor: Eye" or "Eye Doctor." Some professions like Attorneys or Contractors have several specialties. You could list them as a general heading with sub-headings, such as:

> Profession
> Attorney, Real Estate

- ○ Attorney: Personal Injury
- ○ Attorney: Real Estate
- ○ Attorney: Estate Planning
- ○ Attorney: Intellectual Law

Or by their specificity first and general title after:

- ○ Roofing Contractor
- ○ Electrical Contractor
- ○ Carpentry Contractor
- ○ Plumbing Contractor

It is really your own personal judgment call.

3. **Business Name**—their exact company name. If your friend, John Smith, is an attorney and is a sole practitioner, his business name is probably something like, "Johnathan H. Smith, Esq." List all names accurately, so if you have to send something or refer someone to them, they have accurate information. The more organized and accurate information you have on all your networkers, the more professional you look to everyone you refer and refer to. No one wants to call someone and have the name incorrect or mail something and spell the person's name wrong. It makes them look bad, and then you look bad. You want people to almost envy your organization. This will increase their respect for you and your abilities, and make them a more avid supporter of you.

Business Name
Nina A. Johnson, Esq.

NETWORKER'S DAILY ORGANIZER

4. **Business Phone**—include the area code, and if there is a voice mail system with choices, make note of the number sequence. If you know the voice mail system only gives you a certain length of time to speak, note that with, ".30" for 30 seconds, "1" for 1 minute, and so on. One other great bit of information to have is the names of the in-between people you will speak with before you get to your associate. Is there a receptionist, and if so what's this person's name? Does your associate have a secretary, and what is this person's name? This is gold for you. Every time they answer the phone, be polite and say hello. Make them feel that they are as important to you as the person you are calling for. You will be more likely to be put through, and if you don't get through, you will know the real reason. The most valuable people to you in any organization are the people who know the inside scoop.

> Business Phone
> 212-123-4567x231
> .30/Wendy-Sylvia

5. **Business Fax**—if it is the same number as the business phone write "same" so you know it's not a mistake. If you have to call and wait for a tone before you start the fax, write "delay."

> Business Fax
> Same - delay

SUCCESSFUL BUSINESS NETWORKING

6. **Home Street Address**—include number, street, apartment number or suite number.

> Home Street Address
> 333 Old Meadow
> Suite# 455

7. **Home Phone**—include the area code, and if there is a voice mail system with choices, make note of the number sequence. If you know the voice mail system only gives you a certain length of time to speak, note that with, ".30" for 30 seconds, "1" for 1 minute, and so on. Remember to glance at the spouse and child names before calling.

> Home Phone
> 914-345-6789
> 1./box2

8. **Business Street Address**—include exact number, suite number and the floor. Even if the floor is not necessary for mailing, you want to include it so that if you have to give someone the location and/or directions you can be very specific.

> Business Street Address
> 454 Main St.
> (1 block east of P.Ofc.)

NETWORKER'S DAILY ORGANIZER

9. **Pager**—if the pager has a number code which allows you to skip the outgoing message so you can give your message immediately, include it for easy reference. Also make a note if you need to press pound sign (#) or something similar to save your message.

```
Pager
800-111-2222
#7168
```

10. **Mobile**—note if this number is for private use only or for anyone to call on. Many give their mobile numbers out only to specific people. Make sure you are not giving this number to someone who is not welcome to it. "Pvt." for Private, is a good way to note this. If you know the person can only be reached in their car at certain times, then make note of that. "3-4p" for 3:00 - 4:00 P.M. is a good method.

```
Mobile
914-333-4444
Pvt.
```

11. **City, State, Zip (home)**—write out the city, abbreviate the state and include the 4 digit postal code if you know it in addition to the standard 5 digit zip code.

```
City, State, Zip
Hometown, NY
12345-6789
```

SUCCESSFUL BUSINESS NETWORKING

12. **Spouse & Children**—the first names of the spouse and children of your networkers are important to have with you at all times. Developing a relationship with an associate goes a long way when you can get the family behind you as well. Whenever you call an associate, say hello to whomever answers the phone. If you have their names handy, it makes it that much easier to say hello. Even if there are several children in the house, take a guess of one from the names you have, and you've shown a great effort.

```
Spouse & Children
Bill, Jacqueline, Thomas
```

13. **City, State, Zip (business)**—write out the city, abbreviate the state and include the 4 digit postal code, if you know it, in addition to the standard 5 digit zip code.

```
City, State, Zip
New York, NY
11222-3456
```

14. **E-mail**—you can put it all in lower case because it gets read that way.

```
E-mail
nina@aol.com
```

15. **Website Address**—be exact because one mistake could expel you out of this world, through the web and into the oblivion of the net. "Surfing" in space gets pretty old pretty quickly.

Website Address
ninajnsnesq.com

This Address Book system allows you to have all the vital information you need on your Networking Associates with you at all times. The full bios or resumes that you should have on them will be much larger than this, but no other information is really necessary for you to have with you all the time. When you make use of this system you will realize that you are ready not only to contact your associates at any time but, better yet, you are able to refer them to others with all the information necessary. Make sure when you get together with your associates that they see this system you are using. It will impress them and encourage them to do the same. If you can get all your associates on the same effective system that you are using, then you will have increased the likelihood they refer you to others.

PRIORITIZED "TO DO" LIST

If you are one of those people who sits down and makes lists of all the different things you have to do on one page, then this system is great for you. It will allow you to do the same thing in a much more organized and effective fashion.

This "To Do" system allows you to list all of the responsibilities of your many different roles on one master page. Once you have written down your responsibilities in each section, you are then able to transfer the phone calls and things you have to do to the Prioritized Phone Calls and Prioritized Activities boxes on the right side of the page. This allows you to identify the phone calls you have to make and the things you have to do. When you organize your day, you can set aside time to just make phone calls and get them out of the way. When you organize the things you have to do, you do it according to the importance of your priorities. What is great about this page is that it allows you to see all the things you have do each day and know exactly how you are going to attack them. As you accomplish each responsibility, you can check it off and move down the list. The things you couldn't finish that day you move to the next day's "To Do" list in its proper section. Take a look on the next page for an example.

To set it up on your computer, you need to first decide how many different sections you want according to the number of varied responsibilities you have. This can always be changed, so don't get stressed out over it. *Example*: Business, Church/Temple, Little League, Family, Household, Personal and any other groups or activities you may be involved in. Once you know, you can divide the page by using the tables program or in a word processing program. In *Publisher*:

○ Click on the "Tables" icon and pull the table to the length of the page and $\frac{2}{3}$ the width of the page.

○ In the "Create Table" box, put the respective number of rows you need for the number of different sections you wish to have, and put "1" for Columns.

NETWORKER'S DAILY ORGANIZER

TODAY/TOMORROW "TO DO" LIST DATE: _____	PRIORITIZED PHONE CALLS:
BUSINESS	1.
	2.
	3.
	4.
	5.
	6.
	7.
	8.
	9.
	10.
	11.
	12.
	13.
	14.
	15.
CHURCH/TEMPLE	16.
	17.
	18.
	19
	20
	21.
	22.
	23.
FAMILY	24.
	25.

PRIORITIZED ACTIVITIES:

1.
2.
3.
4.
5.
6.
7.
8.
9.
10.
11.
12.
13.
14.
15.
16.
17.
18.
19.
20.
21.
22.
23.
24.
25.

OTHER

PERSONAL

VOLUNTEER ORGANIZATIONS

- For "Table Format" you can choose "None" for now.

- In a word processing program you can count the number of lines on the page and divide it evenly for the number of sections you need.

On the right side of the page you want to put two long text boxes, one on top of the other, for "Prioritized Phone Calls" and "Prioritized Activities." You will be able to adjust these boxes whenever you need to, so for now you can just make them about the same size.

In each section, put the name of the activity in the upper left hand corner. On the very top of the page you should put "Today's/Tomorrow's To Do List," and then further to the right, "Date." This allows you to use this paper for two days, if necessary. You date it so you can file it away later on and always refer back to it. Once you have it set up the way you like it, then you should print out as many copies as you like.

You can either write in the different sections manually or with the computer. Go to each section and write down the different things you have to do, no matter what they are. Don't write them down in any particular order. You are writing in this section now just to get your thoughts organized and down on paper. After you have finished doing this with each section, you should go through each section and make note of what needs to be done first and what can wait. Just number each thing you need to do in each section.

Always start with "1" for each section. You don't want to number the things you have to do in the first section 1 through 10, and then start with 11 in the next section. They are two different sections and need to be prioritized that way. Once you have done this with all the sections,

NETWORKER'S DAILY ORGANIZER

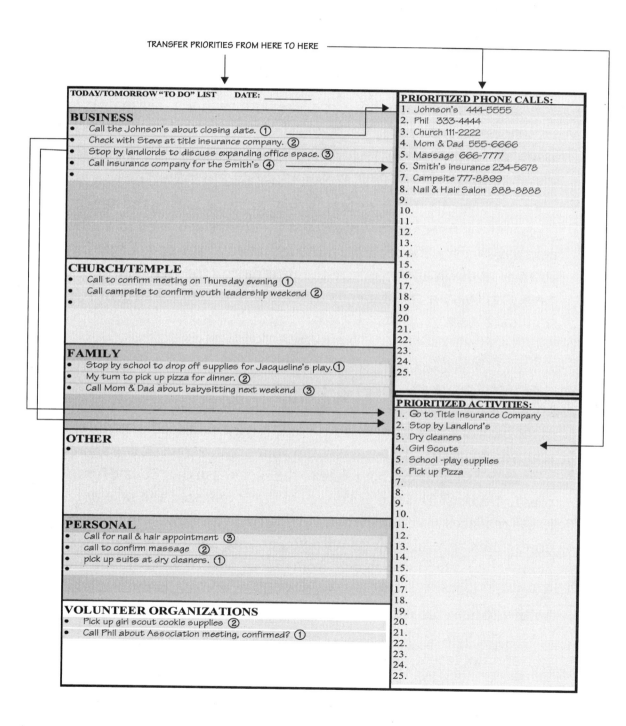

now you need to go back and decide which #1 thing to do in each section is the greatest priority. Take that one and make it #1 in the "Activities" or "Phone Call" section. Do the same with the remaining #1s, and then continue this procedure with each number in every section. By the time you're done, you should have all of your things to do on the left side of the page transferred into one of the two boxes on the right side of the page in order of their importance.

What we love about this system is that, anytime during the day, it gives you the freedom to write down the things you need to do the next day in a specific section on the left; then at the end of that day you can sit down and prioritize the next day on the right side of the page. It allows for spontaneous thought and organized structure, simultaneously.

RESPONSIBILITY NOTE PADS

In the back of your organizer you should have a blank pad that you can remove and use to take notes. Within your organizer itself, you should have note pad sections that relate to the sections in the "Today/Tomorrow To Do List." This is a great way to stay organized and take notes in the respective sections when necessary. This allows you to keep notes about several projects with you at once, all divided into their own section. When you change from one activity to another, you are set up to handle your various responsibilities at once, because all the notes you need are with you. I love it, especially when I get a great idea in the middle of the night. I am able to write it in the related section and not lose it. This is much more efficient than writing on a napkin or on the back of a business card. I think we've all had that experience. Being prepared to capture an idea is as important as the actual implementation of the idea. If you forget the idea before you're able to make note of it, it's probably lost forever or remembered too late.

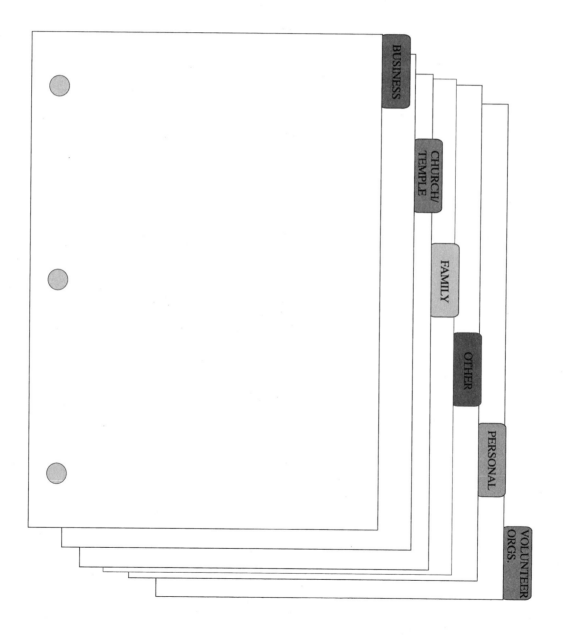

SUCCESSFUL BUSINESS NETWORKING

Creating these sections can be as easy as buying a packet of three-ring binder dividers or dividers that fit your organizer, and then labeling each section alphabetically for your different responsibilities. Put in some lined paper and keep track of each idea and note you put in it by dating each entry you write in the section.

REAL LIFE APPOINTMENT SCHEDULE

Does your day start at 9 A.M. and end at 5 P.M.? I am referring to your day of responsibilities, not just work. This includes: work, house cleaning, food shopping, errands, association and organization meetings, picking up the kids, dinner, etc. Wouldn't you say it is more accurately from 7 A.M. to 9 P.M. by the time you are ready to relax before you go to bed or watch television.

We have never been able to make use of the appointment calendars in other organizers because they just didn't leave space for a long enough day. I don't know about you, but I have "appointments" (a.k.a. responsibilities) well past 5 P.M. The appointment calendar that we made up starts at 7 A.M. and goes until 9 P.M. If I know I'm going to have a crazy week, I will just print out a new one with a longer day on it. I also make the appointment calendar for Monday through Sunday because I have appointments all weekend as well. In fact, sometimes I think that I am busier with my weekend responsibilities than my work week. When I have a relaxing weekend planned, it makes me feel good to look at my weekend calendar and see "Time to relax." It motivates me to get there during midweek. Take a look at the one on the next page for an example.

NETWORKER'S DAILY ORGANIZER

_____WEEK OF_____ OF _____

TIME	MONDAY___	TUESDAY___	WEDNESDAY___	THURSDAY___	FRIDAY___	SATURDAY___	SUNDAY___
7:00am							
7:30am							
8:00am							
8:30am							
9:00am							
9:30am							
10:00am							
10:30am							
11:00am							
11:30am							
NOON							
12:30pm							
1:00pm							
1:30pm							
2:00pm							
2:30pm							
3:00pm							
3:30pm							
4:00pm							
4:30pm							
5:00pm							
5:30pm							
6:00pm							
6:30pm							
7:00pm							
7:30pm							
8:00pm							
8:30pm							
9:00pm							

SUCCESSFUL BUSINESS NETWORKING

- ○ This is easy to set up on your computer with Microsoft Publisher.

- ○ Go to your blank page and pull "Set up the Page" with a full table.

- ○ In "Rows," enter 30, and in "Columns," put 8. This allows you enough rows to have a 7 A.M. to 9 P.M. schedule and put all the days of the week up top.

- ○ Go to the far left column, and put in all the times divided into half-hour time slots all the way down the page.

- ○ In the top box, put "Time," and across that top row, put the days of the week.

_____WEEK OF_____ OF _____							
TIME	MONDAY___	TUESDAY___	WEDNESDAY___	THURSDAY___	FRIDAY___	SATURDAY___	SUNDAY___

- ○ Above the whole chart on the top right put, "_____week of_____of (year)." This way you can print out or copy as many of these as you like and customize them to the month and week. For the first week of January you would put: "1st week of January of 1998."

- ○ In the boxes where the days of the week are, you put a "___" next to each day, and then you can fill in the date.

- ○ You can print or copy these on front and back and save yourself a lot of space in your organizer.

If you know you have a certain responsibility the same time every day or for many days, then fill that in on the computer and it will print out already set. That way you don't have to rewrite the same thing over and over. This is also a good way to commit yourself to things like an exercise routine, reading, family time, etc. If you put them in so it is pre-written before you print it out, you no longer have the excuse of, "I totally forgot because it wasn't written in my organizer." Of course, you may look at this as a disadvantage rather than an advantage.

SHORT- AND LONG-TERM GOALS MASTER SHEET

As we all know, it is important to set goals in everything we do. Whether it's getting the laundry done this Saturday, losing 10 pounds in 10 weeks, or earning over $100,000 a year by a certain age, goals like these allow us to work toward something specific. Setting goals alone isn't the key to achieving them, however. You must have a specific goal and come up with a plan to achieve it.

Let me give you an example. You are a real estate agent and you want to be a million-dollar producer next year. What you need to do is work out how to get there. That means you must find out what the average home in your area is selling for. Take the low side of that average, and make this the price of the homes you are working with. How many of these homes do you need to list and/or sell to reach your goal? Once you have worked out the mathematics, you then must divide that number by the amount of time you are giving yourself to achieve your million-dollar mark. You now have the real number you must make on a monthly basis. What you have done is set a long-term goal and then figured out the short and intermediate goals that you must accomplish in order to achieve it. From your monthly goals you can set weekly and daily goals (i.e., the number of phone calls to make each day, hours spent in the office, etc.) Each of these little goals is a small step to achieving your ultimate goal. As you accomplish the small ones on a daily basis, you gain greater confidence and, therefore, more motivation. The more specific you make your goals—meaning, the more detailed and the more you break them down—the easier it is to achieve them.

This system encourages you to focus on working for something specific. It will keep you motivated and will let you know how you are doing by checking your progress toward your goal daily.

Writing your goals down and referring back to them regularly makes them become real. If you don't write them down and work out a plan on how to achieve them, then they are really just dreams, not goals. Goals start with dreams. Dreams are wonderful. They are what this country is built on. Dreamers made this country. They had a vision of their dream, and then they made a plan and set goals on how to achieve their dream. Without the transference from a dream to a goal, nothing would ever get done. This is what writing them down helps you do. However, writing them down is only the first step. Usually people write their goals down somewhere, like in a diary, and never refer back to them. Others write them down and stick them up in a place they can see them every day, but never update them.

The Short- and Long-Term Goals Master Sheet that we have designed helps you do the following:

1   Set goals for each aspect or responsibility of your life and put them all in one place.

NETWORKER'S DAILY ORGANIZER

2 Set long-term goals, up to 5 years ahead, and periodic short-term goals that allow you to see your progress all on one sheet.

3 Makes you update your progress monthly by rewriting your goals on the set date you decide.

4 Be specific in terms of the exact date each interim goal is to be accomplished.

5 Keep the Master Sheet in your organizer so you can see it every day, at different times of the day.

6 Allows you to never lose track of all the different goals you have in your life.

7 Reminds you of what activity is dominating your life by showing which activities are being ignored and goals that are not being met.

Being an effective networker helps you achieve the goals you have set for yourself. **The 7 Secrets** is the operating and organizational system that allows you to achieve your goals. All the different aspects of this system are designed to make you more effective at building your business, maintaining relationships, prioritizing your life and making sure your energies and time are spent as productively as possible in achieving your goals and maintaining your priorities.

A proper operating system means that you can actually make use of your organizational system. If you find you are constantly in the learning mode of how to use your organizer or are confused by it, then you are not making the best use of your time. The ability to use it with ease is the key. It's one of those thankless jobs. If it is an effective system, you should almost not notice you're using it.

Have you ever been in a restaurant and then realized at the end of the meal how smoothly everything went? You were never in need of something that wasn't there. The plates were removed without being noticed, and you hardly remember the waitstaff even being around except to take the order. This means the job was well done. This is what we mean by a thankless job. When you've been in the restaurant and you can't find the server when you need something, you feel like you are waiting for the meal; and when you are finished it seems that the plates are sitting on the table forever. This means that your server has not been efficient. The job of the restaurant is to provide you with a wonderful night of dining and relaxation. If the servers do their job correctly, you will hardly notice them. If they are too obtrusive or become a focal point of your dining experience, then they have failed at their job.

Your system is the same. You should have a goal-setting system that allows you to focus on your goals and achieve them without even noticing that you are doing it. It shouldn't seem like you are working at it. You should notice how much more free time you have and how many more things you are able to accomplish with much less stress. That is what a proper, effective organizational and operational system should do for you.

To set up your goals sheet:

- Pull down the "Tables" icon, and pull it to full page.

- For number of Rows, put the respective amount you had on your "To Do" list, plus one.

- For Columns, enter 7.

NETWORKER'S DAILY ORGANIZER

75

SET YOUR GOALS AND ACHIEVE THEM!!!

RESPONSI-BILITIES	1 MONTH GOAL DATE _____	3 MONTH GOAL DATE _____	6 MONTH GOAL DATE _____	1 YEAR GOAL DATE	2 YEAR GOAL DATE	5 YEAR GOAL DATE
BUSINESS	•	•	•	•	•	•
CHURCH / TEMPLE	•	•	•	•	•	•
FAMILY	•	•	•	•	•	•
OTHER	•	•	•	•	•	•
PERSONAL	•	•	•	•	•	•
VOLUN-TEER ORGANI-ZATIONS	•	•	•	•	•	•

SUCCESSFUL BUSINESS NETWORKING

○ In the top left hand column, type "Responsibilities."

○ Enter the following column headings in the next 6 columns:

1 Month Goal Date   _____

3 Month Goal Date   _____

6 Month Goal Date   _____

1 Year Goal Date   _____

2 Year Goal Date   _____

5 Year Goal Date   _____

As an added extra we put, "SET YOUR GOALS AND ACHIEVE THEM!!!" at the top of the page, just for a little motivation.

The best way to use this sheet is to start by writing down your long-term goals. We think it is important that you should be thinking in five-year segments for each aspect of your life. It gives you a realistic amount of time to see shorter, interim goals happen so you can keep on track. It is not so far away that it doesn't seem real. As you know, five years pass much more quickly than you would have ever thought. Your long-term goals should be your dreams, desires, passions. If you have a five-year goal to earn a certain amount of money, write it down. If, when earning that money, you want to have a certain type of car, house, boat, then write that down. As we said before, it is important to be specific and to work out specific plans.

Now start working backward on the chart. If you entered a five-year goal, now go to the two- year slot, and write in where you have to be to keep you on track for the five-year goal. Do the same with the other time periods. Will you know exactly where you should be? Very unlikely. The point is to write down these interim goals and update them every month. They will change shape and form. That's good. It means that things are progressing and you have to be willing to adapt to this schedule. When you first write the five-year goal it will seem very far away, almost unrealistic. You will be surprised how quickly it comes up as you are updating your goals on a monthly basis. All of a sudden a year will go by, and then two. Consistency is the key here. Make sure that every month, on the date you have pre-scribed, you update your goals. Your pride, esteem and confidence will be lifted, and you will be motivated for the next month.

VARIOUS CALENDARS

There are so many different calendars you can have. We have organized this section so you can take a look at several calendars to see which combination best fits your needs. You can use them all, or just one or two of them. They are designed to be a complete or self-sustaining system.

Annual Calendar

This allows you to look at the whole year ahead and see what will be happening when. You can use a code to show when certain important dates are coming up. You can do all of this by hand with just a few simple steps.

First, list the different special events you would like marked on your annual calendar. Here are some examples:

○ Family Birthdays

○ Family Anniversaries

- Vacation Time
- Legal Holidays
- Religious Holidays
- Annual Conferences

Next, pick out some symbols you can use to mark each event above. Make sure they are easily recognized and not hard to do by hand. For example:

- Diamond = Religious Holidays
- Circle = Family Anniversaries
- Triangle = Vacation Time
- Lightning = Legal Holidays
- Star = Birthdays
- Starburst = Annual Conferences

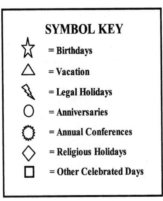

NETWORKER'S DAILY ORGANIZER

If you have more events you want to mark, you can use additional symbols such as check marks or diamonds. Be creative, but make it easy to remember and use. You will be able to see the various events of each month way ahead of time. This will help you organize yourself so you can do what you need to do on time (see page 80).

Dates to Remember

This is another option to keeping track of important dates throughout the year. This particular calendar does not have dates on it, but it provides space to write down what and when the important dates are. It is best to use this calendar in conjunction with the regular annual calendar. It allows you to flip the calendar over and find the particular date marked with its symbol and see the details about that day's event (see page 81).

The best way to do this is to:

○ Go to a blank page, click on the table icon and bring up a two-inch square box about two inches from the top left side of the page.

○ When the table box comes down, choose 7 Rows, 1 Column.

○ In the table format section, click the checkbook register.

○ On the top row of the box type "JANUARY."

○ Repeat this procedure for all twelve months.

○ Arrange the boxes with 3 months across the top and 4 months down.

SUCCESSFUL BUSINESS NETWORKING

1998

SYMBOL KEY
☆ = Birthdays
△ = Vacation
⚡ = Legal Holidays
○ = Anniversaries
⊙ = Annual Conferences
◇ = Religious Holidays
□ = Other Celebrated Days

January
S	M	T	W	T	F	S
				1	2	3
4	5	6	7	8	9	10
11	12	13	14	15	16	17
18	19	20	21	22	23	24
25	26	27	28	29	30	31

February
S	M	T	W	T	F	S
1	2	3	4	5	6	7
8	9	10	11	12	13	14
15	16	17	18	19	20	21
22	23	24	25	26	27	28

March
S	M	T	W	T	F	S
1	2	3	4	5	6	7
8	9	10	11	12	13	14
15	16	17	18	19	20	21
22	23	24	25	26	27	28
29	30	31				

April
S	M	T	W	T	F	S
			1	2	3	4
5	6	7	8	9	10	11
12	13	14	15	16	17	18
19	20	21	22	23	24	25
26	27	28	29	30		

May
S	M	T	W	T	F	S
					1	2
3	4	5	6	7	8	9
10	11	12	13	14	15	16
17	18	19	20	21	22	23
24	25	26	27	28	29	30
31						

June
S	M	T	W	T	F	S
	1	2	3	4	5	6
7	8	9	10	11	12	13
14	15	16	17	18	19	20
21	22	23	24	25	26	27
28	29	30				

July
S	M	T	W	T	F	S
			1	2	3	4
5	6	7	8	9	10	11
12	13	14	15	16	17	18
19	20	21	22	23	24	25
26	27	28	29	30	31	

August
S	M	T	W	T	F	S
						1
2	3	4	5	6	7	8
9	10	11	12	13	14	15
16	17	18	19	20	21	22
23	24	25	26	27	28	29
30	31					

September
S	M	T	W	T	F	S
		1	2	3	4	5
6	7	8	9	10	11	12
13	14	15	16	17	18	19
20	21	22	23	24	25	26
27	28	29	30			

October
S	M	T	W	T	F	S
				1	2	3
4	5	6	7	8	9	10
11	12	13	14	15	16	17
18	19	20	21	22	23	24
25	26	27	28	29	30	31

November
S	M	T	W	T	F	S
1	2	3	4	5	6	7
8	9	10	11	12	13	14
15	16	17	18	19	20	21
22	23	24	25	26	27	28
29	30					

December
S	M	T	W	T	F	S
		1	2	3	4	5
6	7	8	9	10	11	12
13	14	15	16	17	18	19
20	21	22	23	24	25	26
27	28	29	30	31		

DATES TO REMEMBER IN 1998

JANUARY

FEBRUARY

MARCH

APRIL

MAY

JUNE

JULY

AUGUST

SEPTEMBER

OCTOBER

NOVEMBER

DECEMBER

Quarterly

This calendar has 3 months of the year on each page.

○ Page 1—January, February, March

○ Page 2—April, May, June

○ Page 3—July, August, September

○ Page 4—October, November, December

This allows you to look at your schedule for the next 3 months and see what big events are coming up within that quarter. This can be used as its own calendar or in conjunction with the other calendars: Annual, Dates To Remember and Monthly. The Quarterly calendar allows you to note the big events that are marked on the annual calendar and see which important daily events will be happening during that time in greater detail. You can list the two, three or four things you have planned that day, but with no detail. We find this quarterly calendar very useful because of its simplicity and ability to provide enough detail for general scheduling of future events. It takes a little more time to set up on your computer, but once you've done the first one, the other three quarters are as easy as just substituting the numbers and month names:

○ At a blank page, click on the "Table" icon and make the first table at the top of the page, 3½ inches long by 7½ inches wide.

○ At the menu, put 6 Rows and 7 Columns.

○ For Table Format, choose List 6.

NETWORKER'S DAILY ORGANIZER

JANUARY	SUNDAY	MONDAY	TUESDAY	WEDNESDAY	THURSDAY	FRIDAY	SATURDAY
					1	2	3
	4	5	6	7	8	9	10
	11	12	13	14	15	16	17
	18	19	20	21	22	23	24
	25	26	27	28	29	30	31

FEBRUARY	SUNDAY	MONDAY	TUESDAY	WEDNESDAY	THURSDAY	FRIDAY	SATURDAY
	1	2	3	4	5	6	7
	8	9	10	11	12	13	14
	15	16	17	18	19	20	21
	22	23	24	25	26	27	28

MARCH	SUNDAY	MONDAY	TUESDAY	WEDNESDAY	THURSDAY	FRIDAY	SATURDAY
	1	2	3	4	5	6	7
	8	9	10	11	12	13	14
	15	16	17	18	19	20	21
	22	23	24	25	26	27	28
	29	30	31				

SUCCESSFUL BUSINESS NETWORKING

APRIL

SUNDAY	MONDAY	TUESDAY	WEDNESDAY	THURSDAY	FRIDAY	SATURDAY
			1	2	3	4
5	6	7	8	9	10	11
12	13	14	15	16	17	18
19	20	21	22	23	24	25
26	27	28	29	30		

MAY

SUNDAY	MONDAY	TUESDAY	WEDNESDAY	THURSDAY	FRIDAY	SATURDAY
					1	2
3	4	5	6	7	8	9
10	11	12	13	14	15	16
17	18	19	20	21	22	23
24/31	25	26	27	28	29	30

JUNE

SUNDAY	MONDAY	TUESDAY	WEDNESDAY	THURSDAY	FRIDAY	SATURDAY
	1	2	3	4	5	6
7	8	9	10	11	12	13
14	15	16	17	18	19	20
21	22	23	24	25	26	27
28	29	30				

NETWORKER'S DAILY ORGANIZER

JULY	SUNDAY	MONDAY	TUESDAY	WEDNESDAY	THURSDAY	FRIDAY	SATURDAY
				1	2	3	4
	5	6	7	8	9	10	11
	12	13	14	15	16	17	18
	19	20	21	22	23	24	25
	26	27	28	29	30	31	

AUGUST	SUNDAY	MONDAY	TUESDAY	WEDNESDAY	THURSDAY	FRIDAY	SATURDAY
							1
	2	3	4	5	6	7	8
	9	10	11	12	13	14	15
	16	17	18	19	20	21	22
	23/30	24/31	25	26	27	28	29

SEPTEMBER	SUNDAY	MONDAY	TUESDAY	WEDNESDAY	THURSDAY	FRIDAY	SATURDAY
			1	2	3	4	5
	6	7	8	9	10	11	12
	13	14	15	16	17	18	19
	20	21	22	23	24	25	26
	27	28	29	30			

SUCCESSFUL BUSINESS NETWORKING

OCTOBER

SUNDAY	MONDAY	TUESDAY	WEDNESDAY	THURSDAY	FRIDAY	SATURDAY
				1	2	3
4	5	6	7	8	9	10
11	12	13	14	15	16	17
18	19	20	21	22	23	24
25	26	27	28	29	30	31

NOVEMBER

SUNDAY	MONDAY	TUESDAY	WEDNESDAY	THURSDAY	FRIDAY	SATURDAY
1	2	3	4	5	6	7
8	9	10	11	12	13	14
15	16	17	18	19	20	21
22	23	24	25	26	27	28
29	30					

DECEMBER

SUNDAY	MONDAY	TUESDAY	WEDNESDAY	THURSDAY	FRIDAY	SATURDAY
		1	2	3	4	5
6	7	8	9	10	11	12
13	14	15	16	17	18	19
20	21	22	23	24	25	26
27	28	29	30	31		

NETWORKER'S DAILY ORGANIZER

○ On the top row, write in all the days of the week starting with Sunday.

○ Find your most recent calendar and fill in the dates.

○ Repeat this procedure for all the calendars.

Monthly Calendar

Here is a close up of your month and the general day-by-day schedule. By having a full-page calendar of the month, you can put down the different things you have planned each day and the general times you have to do them.

To set this up:

○ Pull down the "Tables" icon and bring it to a full page.

○ At the "Create Tables" box, enter 6 Rows and 7 Columns. Reduce the top row to only a half inch wide. You will use this for labeling the days of the week.

○ Enter the days of the week, beginning with Sunday, in the upper left box.

○ Now enter your days of the week according to the recent year's calendar.

○ After you have finished, pull a text box to the upper right side of the calendar and make it large enough (about 14 point) to easily read the month.

SUCCESSFUL BUSINESS NETWORKING

JANUARY

SUNDAY	MONDAY	TUESDAY	WEDNESDAY	THURSDAY	FRIDAY	SATURDAY
				1	2	3
4	5	6	7	8	9	10
11	12	13	14	15	16	17
18	19	20	21	22	23	24
25	26	27	28	29	30	31

Part III

EVALUATION

SECRET 2:

TAKE A "NAPP" AND GET
MORE REFERRALS

Chapter 6

EVALUATE YOUR NETWORKERS

NETWORKER ASSOCIATE PARTICIPATION PROGRAM (NAPP)

In a previous chapter, you organized everyone you know into your 5 Networker Categories. Now we want you to think of each person and recall just what they have been doing for you. Your results will let you know how much work you have to do, in terms of developing networking relationships with your associates, so you can increase the amount and quality of help you are receiving from them. The Networker Associate Participation Program (NAPP) is something you will want to keep updated so you know how you are doing and where you need to concentrate your energies.

With any system you use in business, you need to be able to dissect it and see if it is working. If you can't track your progress, then you'll never know if the system is working at full efficiency. After you have completed your initial NAPP and if you keep it updated, it will be easy to track what your associates are doing for you, and you for them. This is crucial to the success of your networking system.

WHAT HAVE YOU BEEN GETTING, IF ANYTHING?

Now that you have finished organizing your networking categories, the next step is to evaluate just what you have been getting from your Networking Associates. As we do this, if you find that you have been getting very little from your Networking Associates, don't be disappointed. Everyone is pretty much the same. The purpose of this book is to make you a more effective and successful networker. To do this you need to organize your associates and put together an operating system that is going to work. Before we are able to do that, we must first see where you are at so we can design the precise program that can get you where you want to be.

FOUR TYPES OF HELP

There are four types of help your Networking Associates can give you:

1   **Information**—any business-related information that your associate learns about that might be of interest to you, such as: chamber mixers; vertical market trade shows (all one industry)

like a computer trade show or a wedding trade show; or horizontal trade shows (many professions represented) like a home owners' trade show or business trade show; future tax laws; new government regulations, etc.

2   **Contacts**—a contact is made when you are looking for someone at a specific company to contact, and one of your Networking Associates knows a person who works there or knows of a person that works there. A contact would mean that I give you a name, but using my name would not do any good.

A few weeks ago a friend called me up and asked if I knew of a local police officer that would be interested in volunteering time to fingerprint some children for a child identification program they were running. I found one in my mailing list. A few years earlier I had received a card from a police officer at a children's program. I gave my friend the name but told her that he would not know who I was. It gave her a contact, but my name wasn't going to do her any good. However, having a name to ask for and a particular person to speak with is much more powerful than calling and asking the desk sergeant for a volunteer. If someone asks for you by name, they got it from somewhere, so you tend to feel a little more obliged to respond.

3   **Connections**—a connection is the next step up from a contact. You may be looking for someone at a company. If I know the person and they know me, I would tell you to call the person and use my name. This would help you get your foot in the door.

If you were a carpet cleaner and wanted to clean the carpets in a certain restaurant and hadn't been able to contact the owner, and if I knew her, I would give you her name and tell you to use my name: "Tell her I told you to call." This is much stronger than a contact, yet not quite a referral.

I was at an association meeting, and one of my colleagues told me he was looking to do business with a relatively new company that needed to reorganize in order to get to the next level—a company that was making between one and 20 million dollars per year. He would be able to help them reorganize. He was an acquaintance of mine, and I had heard that he did good work. Nevertheless, I didn't feel comfortable calling the company I was thinking of and promoting him, but I did give him the name of the president of the company and told him to use my name. The president of the company called me after they talked on the phone and asked me for my input. I explained that I had no personal experience with the gentleman I connected him with, but that I had heard good things about him. He appreciated my honesty and I asked him to let me know how things turned out.

4   **Referrals**—a referral is the next step up. In all of the other instances listed above, the person I am helping makes the initial contact. In a referral, I will make the initial contact for you. I give your name to someone, help sell you, and tell them that you will give them a call. They are expecting your phone call and have already received a testimonial from me about you. There are different levels of referrals which we will discuss in the next section.

Now that we understand the difference between the four types of help your Networking Associates can give you, we need to evaluate just what kind of help you have been getting.

Initially, you really only need to do this with your Primary and Secondary Networking Associates. The rest aren't regular contacts, but you will have exceptions. Put a sheet together with five columns, labeled: Name, Information, Contacts, Connections, Referrals. Start at the top of your Primary Network (see page 96).

As you go down your list and find people who have helped you, put their names on your new list and write down how they helped you. If you're not exactly sure, guesstimate. Again, this will give you an idea of who in your network is really active and who is not.

THREE LEVELS OF REFERRALS

Referrals are the best people we can meet through our associates on a regular basis. However, there are three different levels of referrals:

1   Simple Referrals—No energy spent getting a referral

2   Compound Referrals—

    A. Heard a need, gave a referral

    B. Recognized future needs, gave a referral

3   Complex Referrals—Used their own networks to help you

Simple Referral

A Simple Referral is the most fundamental of the three. When you first establish a networking relationship with a new associate, they will usually use your product or service themselves or refer you to someone who directly asks them to recommend a person in your profession. These

SUCCESSFUL BUSINESS NETWORKING

NAME	INFORMATION	CONTACTS	CONNECTIONS	REFERRALS

referrals are by no means less valuable than the other two, they are just easier for your associate to give to you. "Simple" refers to the amount of time and energy spent getting you the referral. At this stage associates will not go out of their way to refer you to someone. In this case, the referral is not initiated by your associate but by the person who is in need of assistance.

Example: A friend of yours tells you she is looking for a financial planner and asks if you know a good one. You say yes and refer the one in your network.

Compound Referrals

Compound referrals occur when you have established a solid networking relationship with your associates. They understand how they can help find a referral for you. The main difference between Compound and Simple Referrals is that your associate initiates the process. It is the difference between a referral falling in their lap for you and actively finding a need for your product or service.

There are actually two different levels of Compound Referrals:

1 Recognized a current need and gave a referral

   Example: You are having a conversation with one of your networking associates, and he mentions that he is planning to computerize his whole office in the next couple of months. You tell him that before he does anything, he should speak with your computer consultant.

2 Recognized a future need and gave a referral

Example: A friend of yours just got married, and you tell him that if he is planning on buying a home in the next couple of years, he should start to plan now. You put him in contact with a financial planner, a mortgage broker and a good accountant. This allows him to plan ahead for the type of home he wants and how he's going to get it. You are able to refer three people in your network.

Complex Referrals

Complex Referrals occur when your associates truly go out of their way to help you find what you need. They will call the people they know and ask these contacts to help them find what you are looking for. They must sell you to the contacts with whom they have a strong relationship. This level of networking will not happen until you have proven to your associate why they should go out of their way for you. In networking, this is achieved by building strong relationships with your associates and consistently helping them.

Example: You're a consultant, and you know one of the major corporations that you have been trying to get into is accepting bids for a consulting contract. You know you would be right for the job, but you are not one of the invited companies. You call me and ask if I know of anyone who can open the door for you. I call a friend of mine, and he calls a friend of his, and we are able to get you an invitation to bid on the contract.

I have used my contacts and my network to help you. This is the ultimate referral and the hardest to develop.

Any referral you get from your Networking Associates is worth a great deal to you. It doesn't matter if it is a Simple, Compound or

Complex Referral. If someone is referring you, they obviously believe in you and your capabilities. The reason you want to evaluate the three different types of referrals is so you can work on developing deeper relationships. The stronger your relationship with your networker, the greater the distance they are willing to go for you.

THE PRIMARY-COMPLEX RELATIONSHIP

Take out a piece of paper and write down how many people you know who would be willing to put their careers on the line for you. If there were a business opportunity and I said to these people, "I'm considering (your name) for this opportunity. I am going to leave the decision up to you. If he works out I will reward you; if he doesn't, you will be to blame and you will be finished. Or you could tell me to ask someone else for a recommendation." How many people do you know who would put their reputation on the line for you? How many people have 100 percent full faith in you and believe in you and all of your capabilities? How many people would you do that for?

You probably didn't need to write this down because the number is probably pretty low. It is the same for just about everyone. The people we are talking about are those we are closest to—mother, father, sisters, brothers, relatives, best friends, business partners—not many others. These are the people in your Primary Network who would give you Complex Referrals. They would be willing to put their reputations on the line for you and call on other people in their network to help you. This Primary-Complex relationship is the ideal relationship we would like to establish with all of our Networking Associates. It is not realistic that this will happen, but it is what we are always striving for. We want to continuously move people up in our Networking Categories toward the Primary and improve our referrals to the Complex. In the diagram on the next page you can see the average percentage of Simple, Compound and Complex Referrals at each Networking Category level. As you can see, the greatest percentage of Complex Referrals happen in the Primary level; the least happen in the Inactive level.

In order to increase the value of our networks, we need to increase the amount and the quality of the help we are receiving from them. Even though help may come in terms of information, contacts, connections or referrals, the referrals are what we want more of. Referrals translate into dollars of profit, which is the ultimate goal of business networking. The only way to know if our networking is working is by evaluating those referrals on a regular basis.

CHART YOUR REFERRALS

Use a sheet broken into six columns (see page 102):

1 Name

2 Networking Level

3 Date

4 Simple

5 Compound

6 Complex

EVALUATE YOUR NETWORKERS

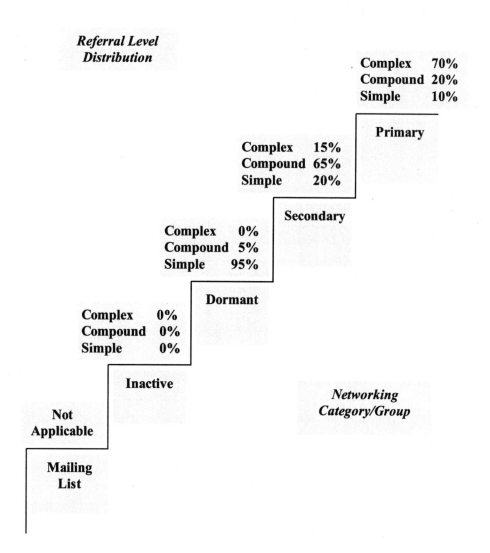

SUCCESSFUL BUSINESS NETWORKING

NAME	NET. LEVEL	DATE	SIMPLE	COMPOUND	COMPLEX
Robert Staskel	P	3/1/98			Donald Trump

EVALUATE YOUR NETWORKERS

Now use the same procedures as before. Go down your list of Primary and Secondary networkers and mark who has given you what type of referral. If possible, make note of when they gave you the referrals, how often and how many. If you are able to do this, then you will develop a system that will allow you to evaluate your networkers and yourself in the future. Out of the referrals you have received, it is important to mark where they have been coming from: your Primary, Secondary or Dormant networks.

Part IV

RESEARCH

SECRET 3:

LOOK INSIDE BEFORE
GOING OUTSIDE

Chapter 7

TAKE A LOOK IN THE MIRROR

In his best-selling book, *The 7 Habits of Highly Effective People*, Steven R. Covey relates the stories of many individuals who have achieved "success" in the eyes of the world but who nevertheless feel empty or unfulfilled. Perhaps you've experienced those feelings yourself that "there has to be more to life than this." Whatever "this" may be might differ for each person, but as human beings there is within each of us an innate desire to find meaning in our lives and in what we do. As social beings we tend to derive that sense of meaning primarily through interrelationships with others.

Each of us tends to believe that we view the world objectively, that the way we see the world is the way it truly is. By and large we tend to think that "my way" is the right way of doing things. In reality, we see the world as we are conditioned to see it. We have preferences that cause us to act in particular ways. For example, fold your hands. Now look at which of your thumbs is on top–right or left. Then unfold you hands and refold them so that the other thumb is on top. It's uncomfortable, right? If you were to do this exercise with a group of people and ask which thumb "belongs" on top, you would get two different answers–and both would be correct. What is "right" for you may not be right for the next person. Since networking is about relationships, we can become more effective networkers by improving our relationships. But we can't improve our relationships without first improving ourselves. In other words, we have to look inside before going outside.

According to Covey, highly effective people have seven habits in common. He says that a person's character is basically a composite of his or her habits, and that a habit is the intersection of knowledge, skill and desire. To Covey, knowledge is "the what to do and the why to do it," skill is the "how to do it," and desire is the motivation, "the want to do it." In order to make something a habit in our lives, we must have all three–knowledge, skill and desire. To be a more effective networker means making networking and relationship building part of our very essence or character: in other words, a habit.

In the model developed by Covey, the seven habits of highly effective people are divided into three categories. The first three habits help a person to become more independent. We can't improve our relationships with others until we improve ourselves and become responsible for our lives. The next three habits are focused outward and help us to become interdependent with other people. The final habit helps us to maintain balance in our lives. Now let's look at these habits and how we can apply them to networking.

HABIT 1—BE PROACTIVE

Reactive people respond to occurrences in their lives based on feelings. They tend to feel that "things happen" to them and that they are victims of circumstances, conditions or their environment. Reactive people tend to sit back and wait. Proactive people, on the other hand, make things happen. They realize that they have the freedom to choose their response to events. In other words, they see themselves not only as responsible, but as "response-able," i.e., as having choices and options in life, of being able to respond to events in a manner of their own choosing.

Proactive people realize that there are some things in life over which they have no control (for example, tomorrow it is going to rain), but they do have the power to choose their responses to those events ("I'm singin' in the rain"). Being proactive means focusing your time and energy on things you can do something about. Or, in the words of the famous Serenity Prayer, "Lord, help me to accept the things I cannot change, the courage to change the things I can, and the wisdom to know the difference."

In networking, not everything will always go your way. You may find yourself giving several referrals to one member of your network who never seems to reciprocate. Or you may find yourself receiving a lot of referrals, but none of them develop into new business. It is in your response to these situations that you have the power to do something about them. For example, maybe you have not been clear enough in defining your business or in identifying the types of referrals you are seeking. So instead of automatically seeking to blame the other party, look inside first. Likewise, the reason the referrals may not be developing into new business could be due to the proposals you have been submitting rather than in the weakness of the referrals. It is by working on yourself and improving your response-ability that you can influence the conditions or circumstances that come along. You get nowhere by blaming or complaining.

HABIT 2—BEGIN WITH THE END IN MIND

An activity we have used in some of our training programs involves having the participants imagine themselves at their own funeral three years in the future. We ask them to write down what they would like to have said about them during their eulogy by four different speakers—a member of their family, a friend, a coworker, and a member of their church or temple. Why not try it for yourself? How would you like to be remembered? What difference would you like to have made in the lives of other people?

You have the power to write the script of your own life. Success lies not in accumulating things but in having mastery over your life. Once you realize that you are in charge, you can set about to live your life in a way that will make you proud to be remembered.

Effective networkers can apply this awareness to their dealings with other people, and therefore, they are continuously seeking opportunities to do things for others. As such, people are much more willing to do things for them in return. Remember, as we have told you before, when it comes to networking, givers get.

HABIT 3—PUT FIRST THINGS FIRST

Habits 1 and 2 deal with doing the right things. Habit 3 is about doing things right. Effective people and successful networkers think preventively. It is not that they are problem minded; rather they are opportunity minded. When mistakes happen, as they will, remember to put first things first. Look for the opportunities to learn and grow from your mistakes rather than lamenting your misfortune. Do not allow other people to set expectations for you or in your life. Frustration results from failure to meet expectations. If you set your own expectations rather than trying to "keep up with the Jonses," you will have far less frustration and much more of a sense of fulfillment in your life.

The key to keeping first things first is not to prioritize what's on your schedule, but rather to schedule your priorities. Only you can determine what is most important in your life. By prioritizing in compliance with your own value system, you can achieve a sense of independence and control and can build your network accordingly. By knowing what is important to you, you can use this knowledge to add people to your network who will help you achieve your goals.

HABIT 4—THINK WIN/WIN

In any interaction or negotiation between human beings, there are six possible outcomes: I win/you win (win/win); I win/you lose (win/lose); I lose/you win (lose/win); we both lose (lose/lose); I win no matter what; and no deal (we agree to disagree). To the person who views life as a win/win proposition, human interaction is based on cooperation rather than competition. As we have said all along, the key to successful networking is to have both parties win by establishing a cooperative relationship.

To achieve to a win/win situation, use this four-step process:

1 See the problem or situation from the other party's point of view.

2 Identify the actual issues and concerns that are involved.

3 Determine what results would be fully acceptable to both of you.

4 Identify possible options to achieve those results.

This win/win philosophy is the first step toward developing interdependency between you and the members of your network. The first three habits will help you to develop a sense of independence. In other words, you can't fully be "you" or enter into a relationship with anyone else until you know who you are. Interdependence comes about as a result of two mature and independent persons deciding to enter into a relationship where they can rely on one another. Interdependence is a far cry from dependence, which implies an immature needing rather than an adult decision. For a win/win proposition to work, each party must possess:

○ Integrity, that they place a high value on themselves

○ Maturity, which is the balance between courage and consideration

○ A mind set that recognizes that there is enough to go around

Effective networkers truly believe that they deserve referrals and new business coming their way. They also strike a balance between assertiveness and altruism; in other words, they want what's best for both themselves and the members of their network, and effective networkers

HABIT 5—SEEK FIRST TO UNDERSTAND, THEN TO BE UNDERSTOOD

know that there is certainly enough business for everybody, especially if everybody in the network works to assist one another.

If you could improve one skill in your life, we would suggest that you focus on improving your communication skills. Interpersonal communication is by far the most important skill in life, and it begins by first trying to understand the other person. In Chapter 12 we discuss the importance of active listening. Unfortunately, when most people listen, it is not with a desire to understand the problem or situation from the speaker's point of view, but to simply gather enough information to enable them to jump in with a solution. How often have you been speaking to someone and realized that they were ignoring you and not really listening at all? Other people pretend to listen by commenting, "Uh-huh," and "Right" every once in a while during your discourse. Others are masters at selective listening (we can probably all occasionally plead guilty to this one when we hear only what we want to hear). With luck and practice you may occasionally run into someone who actually pays attention to what you are saying. But only very rarely in life will we find an emphatic listener, that is, someone who listens to try to understand where you're coming from.

Knowing how to understand another person and communicating so that you can be understood is critical in reaching win/win solutions. Seeking to understand another person requires consideration and commitment on your part. Seeking to be understood requires you to have courage since you will be exposing yourself to the possibility of rejection from the other party. By demonstrating that you really want to understand the needs and the personalities of your networkers before you ask them to understand you, you will be well on the way to having a mature, interdependent relationship.

HABIT 6—SYNERGIZE

The word synergy may sound high falootin,' but it simply means that the whole is greater than the sum of its parts. For example, if I take a board and suspend it between two cinder blocks to serve as a shelf, it will support a certain amount of weight without breaking. If I were to take two boards of the same thickness and put them together between the two cinder blocks, together they would support far more than twice the weight of what two single boards could support. Your network is similar because, together, your skills and attributes and your products and services, combined with your networkers, are a far more intriguing package and certainly a stronger marketing group than any of you could be on your own.

The essence of synergy is to appreciate and capitalize on the differences in people. That is why we have encouraged you to diversify your networks. Remember, as we said in Habit 1, people see the world not as it is, but as they perceive it to be. The perceptions of your networkers are as valid as any perceptions you might hold, and chances are they will be able to see opportunities for you where you might never even imagine them to be.

HABIT 7—BALANCED SELF-RENEWAL

If you were to take an inventory of your business and list all of the assets on one side of the paper and all of the liabilities on the other, which asset would you list first? Balanced self-renewal means preserving and enhancing your greatest asset–yourself.

Peace of mind and self-effectiveness come about only when you live your life in harmony with your true inner values. As the old saying goes, "You can't be good to anyone else if you're not good to yourself." You can't be effective in your relationships or your networking unless you strive to develop balance in your life. Balance means taking care of yourself and your physical, emotional, spiritual and mental needs. In reality and in fact, you become what you tell yourself you are. Listen to the words and the way you describe yourself. Look in the mirror and see the image you project. Look inside before going outside.

Effective and successful networking requires an integration of the seven habits. You must become proactive (Habit 1) and seek out opportunities for networking. If you begin with the end in mind (Habit 2), you can write the script for your personal and professional life, and you can manage your life more effectively and efficiently if you put first things first (Habit 3). Establishing and managing your networks to result in win/win solutions (Habit 4) and seeking first to understand the needs of your networkers (Habit 5) leads to synergy (Habit 6). Self-renewal (Habit 7) is the process of renewing yourself so that you can practice the habits of being an effective networker. Relationships are built from the inside out.

Chapter 8

FIND OUT WHICH NETWORKERS ARE MISSING

YOUR PRIMARY "NET" HAS HOLES, BIG ONES

If you're like 99 percent of the population, your Primary Network has big holes of missing professions that you need. Generally there are two main areas you will get business from. The first is called your **Business Referral Sources (BRS)** and is made up of your **Direct Business Networks (DBN)** and your **Indirect Business Networks (IBN)**. The second is called your **Outside Business Referral Sources (OBRS)** which is made up of your **Various Social Networks (VSN)**. Your BRSs are what we are going to concentrate on in this chapter.

Business Referral Sources (BRS) are other professionals that refer business to yours because of a direct or indirect relationship that they have with you. Let me explain. If I were a real estate attorney, the businesses or professions that would be part of my DBN would include a Realtor, mortgage broker, home inspector, land surveyor, engineer, contractor and architect. All of these professions are related to buying real estate and/or altering that real estate in some way. If, as a real estate attorney, I had all of these people in my DBN, I could refer business to them on a regular basis, and they could refer business to me on a regular basis. Your DBNs serve as a powerful source of constant business to you. If you're not sure which other professions could be in your DBNs, think of professions that you would like to have a relationship with and that you would be able to get regular referrals from, not businesses that would serve as clients but whose clients could be a natural referral to you. Then think of what businesses you could naturally refer business to. Make a list of all these businesses. They comprise the first group you should attempt to include in your network.

Above we also mentioned your Indirect Business Networks (IBN). These are the businesses that you are in contact with or would like to be in contact with just because. For instance, if I am a real estate attorney, I have no direct relationship to a printer, but I would like to know that I have a good one available to me. I might want to include a printer in my IBN so I have someone I can rely on, and when the opportunity arrives, I can refer business to them. Will this printer have any direct business for me? Probably not. But I don't think it would bother him any to know that he has an ace in the hole when it comes to needing a real estate attorney. Plus, he may find someone to refer my way.

FIND OUT WHICH NETWORKERS ARE MISSING

Have you ever played or seen competitive archery? These athletes aim for a bull's eye target with a yellow circle in the center worth 10 points, which is encircled by a red ring worth 8 points, a blue ring worth 5 points and a black ring worth 1 point. I think this is a good metaphor for the business professions you currently have in your networks. What you want to do is to put as many of the professions that would be a 10 in your bull's eye area into your Primary Network. Your DBNs make up your bull's eye. The more 10s you have, the better you are doing.

There are two places you can get your missing networkers from: your current internal networkers and new networkers who you haven't met yet. We want to pull people from one of your internal networking categories before we go outside because we already have a relationship with them. It is much easier to reestablish a relationship and move it up in your networking levels than it is to create a new one and develop that sense of trust and rapport.

When I bought my house, the real estate agent recommended an attorney, a mortgage broker, a title insurance person, a home inspector, a pest control person, an architect and a debris removal person. Was I appreciative? You better believe it. I didn't have to look in the yellow pages or worry about getting ripped off. They all came with the agent's endorsement. That was good enough for me. It made her look more professional in my eyes because she was so well connected. In return I have referred business to her with my endorsement of, "She knows everyone you will need, and they are all good. She will take the work out of buying a home." That is what having a strong DBN can do for you.

When you go to list your DBNs, be a little creative. Don't just go for immediate businesses that come to mind. Anticipate problems or questions your clients might have, and see if you can resolve those problems by having a professional at your disposal who could deal with that type of question.

Let's say that I am a financial planner. I am sitting down with you working out a long-term retirement plan. In my DBN I have an accountant, an attorney, a banker, a mortgage broker and a real estate agent. But I also have an appraiser, a contractor, a landscaper and a pool builder. Do these professions relate directly to what I do? Not at first glance, but if I think about long-term investments for my client, I discover how they could increase the value of their home over the years: maybe a new pool, a modern kitchen or bath, fencing or landscaping. By having these professions at my disposal, I can provide a projection of added value to the home. This helps my client increase the value of one of their most valuable assets, therefore increasing their net worth. This may mean a larger sale for me and a referral for my DBN associates. I end up looking great because I found a way to increase the value of my clients in an unconventional way, at no risk to them. Talk about a win/win situation.

RESCUE THE NETWORKERS THAT YOU DO HAVE

Now that you have targeted your DBNs we can put them aside and be more general. Look through all of the people in your five categories and see what professions they represent. More importantly, look for those people that you feel you had a good relationship with before but have just been out of touch with for a while. You probably went through this when you were listing them in your networks earlier: "Wow, I forgot about her. I should really give her a call." This is what I call your upper 10 percent. Find the top 10 percent of each category and put them into a separate list. You can make this your rescue list. Before they drop down to your Mailing List or into oblivion within your Mailing List, you are going to rescue them and bring them up to your Secondary or Primary Network.

Reestablishing old relationships is not only valuable to your future but quite enjoyable. When you get together you can reminisce about old times and just play catch-up. It will mean a lot to your old friend or business associate that you called and took the initiative to rebuild a relationship. It lets them know that you consider them an important part of your life. This will build their self-esteem and increase their estimation of you as a person and professional.

Each person you call slowly but surely adds to your network. Are they in the profession that you need? Do they have the contacts that you need? Who cares. You are not reestablishing relationships with these people just because of what they do or who they know. You are doing it because you think they are good people and would like to see if, in the future, there is a way for you to help them, and, if the opportunity arises, for them to help you. Don't get me wrong, if you choose to rescue one of the people in your network because of what they do, there is nothing wrong with that. But if they are in the profession you need and you don't like them, don't even bother. If you don't like them, there must be a valid reason, and this means you will not feel comfortable recommending them to someone. If you can't refer them, they will probably not refer you. Move on to someone with whom you could have a mutually beneficial relationship. You're choosing the upper 10 percent of each group as a place to start. Eventually you will want to do this with as many people in your Dormant, Inactive and Mailing List networks as possible. The upper 10 percent is a good place to start because most of these people will be happy to hear from you and to reestablish that prior relationship. It allows you a quick and easy way to build your network.

So how do you do this?

There are two things to work on as you improve your networks. One is to move people up in your networks. The other is to increase the amount of higher level referrals from each person in each level of the network. For instance, in our Primary Network we may increase the number of people in that network from 75 to 100, but how is the quality of the referrals in that network? If only 50 percent of your referrals are complex, then we want to increase that to 55 percent, then to 60 percent, 70 percent,

90 percent, etc. The idea is to always improve our networks. How do we do this? The simple answer is by having a process for building relationships with each member of your networking groups.

The Process:

1   Start with your Secondary Network and find the people who you could easily move up. Maybe there is an associate who you talk to consistently every 8 or 10 weeks. Give her a call and ask her to lunch.

2   At lunch get to know her better. Ask questions about business, family, hobbies, etc. Show your sincere interest, but make sure you are not prying.

3   Explain that the reason you wanted to get together is because you consider her an important part of your network: "There are not many people that I feel comfortable enough to refer business to and offer my help and services in any way I can. We've been friends and business associates for quite some time and I would like to find out what I can do to help you. One of the things I really would like to know more about is your business. Who do you consider a good client? Is there anything I can do to help you to expand your business?"

At no time is there a mention of what I would like you to do for me. That is not what this is about. You want to prove yourself to your associate as a true resource. If they believe you are sincere, they will naturally want to help you too. They will want to give back what you are giving them. They will ask you how they can help you. If they don't, don't worry. It will come in time. You are not getting together with this person so you can get something from them tomorrow. You're establishing a long-term effective network that you will be able to call on in the future for any reason. Long-term success is important in your network. It translates into long-term business and long-term security for your personal life.

4 Follow up your meeting with a card or letter that sincerely states your appreciation and excitement about this new enhanced relationship.

5 Keep in contact every six weeks, at least.

6 Get as much information as you can: your associate's birthdays, anniversaries, family, hobbies, etc.

7 Show them how important they are to you by remembering these things and celebrating with them by card, fax, phone, etc.

Part V

PART V: SKILLS DEVELOPMENT

SECRET 4:

NETWORKERS ARE MADE, NOT BORN

Chapter 9

The Traits of Successful Networkers

Are you a leader or a manager? Managers make systems work, but leaders make things happen. Being a good networker is very similar to being a good leader. Understanding the difference between managing and leading, between old, outdated marketing techniques and harnessing the power of word-of-mouth marketing through networking, will mean the difference between winning and losing in today's highly competitive markets. Successful networkers, like great leaders, make the people around them better. Thus far in this book we have provided you with tips and techniques that clarify the process of networking. It is what you do with this process that will make you successful. The following traits are shared by top leaders and top networkers:

- Stand up for yourself

  If you are not willing to stand up for your own goals and beliefs, no one will do it for you. Wishy-washy people don't make good leaders or networkers. People are attracted to those who know when and how to exercise authority. Let people know that you value them and the opportunities they represent for both of you, and they will line up to follow you.

- Motivate others

  You cannot mandate someone to join your network or command them to provide you with referrals. If you don't like to motivate people, and if you aren't thrilled by the challenge of getting them to give their best, you'll have a tough road ahead as a networker. Great networkers get a real sense of satisfaction out of motivating other people to do better. They want to see others succeed. If your Networking Associates think of you as a person who really motivates them, they will look forward to getting together with you as frequently as possible. And, by convincing other people that they have the ability to perform better, they will develop a strong desire to want to help you to do better likewise.

- Identify with the hits and home runs, not with the strikeouts

  Most baseball players who make it into the Baseball Hall of Fame rarely succeed more than once out of every three times they come to the plate. Even Babe Ruth, who for many years led the major leagues in home runs, also led the major leagues in strikeouts. Not everyone you invite into your network or whose network you

THE TRAITS OF SUCCESSFUL NETWORKERS

129

would like to join will accept the offer. Many of your contacts will never move up into a higher category. In fact, the majority of your networkers may never provide you with a successful referral. Strong leaders and networkers have the sort of egos that allow them to maintain their optimism and to move on to the next opportunity. Likewise, not every referral you give to the people in your network will be successful for them. Successful networkers help other people to bounce back from rejection. Rejection is a part of life, both in social and business situations. You can learn from your mistakes without focusing on them. If you remain positive, so will your networkers.

○ Be willing to take risks

In a competitive marketplace the winners are generally those who are willing to take risks to achieve their goals. Sticking to the tried and true ways of doing things is no longer the safe bet. The world will pass by those who are averse to taking chances. Getting out of your comfort zone and meeting new people is risky. You face the threat of rejection and may even make a fool of yourself. Remember, however, that the only true failure lies in never having tried. If you don't make contacts, and if you don't develop and utilize networkers, you will surely fail. If you do try—sure, you may strike out—but you are just as likely to hit a home run. You will never hit a home run if you don't step up to the plate and swing the bat.

○ Be innovative

Being innovative goes hand in hand with being a risk-taker. Approaching the next millennium, you have to be open to new ideas and new ways of doing things. The world is simply not the same as it was—indeed it is ever changing faster and faster. You cannot afford to go it alone. In an ever-shrinking world and an increasingly competitive marketplace, you need as many people in your personal sales force as possible. Of all the existing marketing techniques, there are only two that directly impact your bottom line—cold calling and word-of-mouth marketing. I'm sure you can think of innovative ways to do both, but only word-of-mouth marketing (i.e., networking) will allow you to reach hundreds or thousands of people even while you're sleeping.

○ Do it now

In today's customer-driven marketplace everyone talks about the importance of urgency, but few people really have it. A sense of urgency separates superior networkers from average networkers. Waiting until tomorrow or until the time is right to make that call or to follow up with one of your networkers opens the door for your competitors. If you let people know that you are willing to go the extra mile or to get on the phone early in the morning or stay late in the evening to accommodate them, they will not only recognize that you think they are important, but they, too, will then develop a sense of urgency. When it comes time for them to give you a referral or to make an introduction for you, you don't want them to drag their feet. Be careful, however, not to treat everything as an emergency. You want to have a sense of urgency without placing yourself under constant stress. Successful leaders and networkers have learned a sense of balance which complements their desire to do it now.

THE TRAITS OF SUCCESSFUL NETWORKERS **131**

○ Empathize with your networkers

Leaders and networking pros are tough, driven and daring, but they also have a heart. Truly successful networkers possess as much compassion as competitive spirit. Be an advocate for your networkers. Understand and relate to them as people, not tools. Realize that the people in your network want to help you every bit as much as you want to help them. Don't beat them up for their mistakes—maybe the blame lies with you and how you have described yourself and your needs to them. Treat the people in your network in such a way that they understand that you are looking out for their best interests, and they will do the same for you.

○ To be a successful networker, be a great leader. To be a great leader, be an effective networker.

NETWORKER ATTRIBUTES

So, what are the skills required to be a good networker? Networking gurus themselves have been discussing these attributes for years. The conclusion is that there is not one and only one profile; but there are certain common characteristics that tend to correlate with success in networking. Based on our interviews and our own experience, the key characteristics may be summarized in the following ten traits:

1 **Integrity**—giving and receiving referrals can affect the lives of many people, including employees, investors and customers. With vested interests at stake, some people will seek to influence your thinking and may try to sway your recommendations. Thus your integrity must remain scrupulous to avoid

the loss of objectivity caused by catering to the demands of any one person or group over another. Any diminishment of your integrity can harm others and yourself.

2 **Salesmanship**—the businessperson who waits for clients to beat a path to his door will soon be out of business. Regardless of the nature of your business, you must sell your services. It is very easy to fall into the trap of spending all of your time on the project at hand, only to come to realize that you have no work to do once that assignment has ended. Wise businesspeople try to schedule assignments to avoid this feast or famine cycle. Selling begins with contacting a person who might be a prospect for your network. Selling is the focus of your discussions with the customer, is crucial at the proposal stage, must be maintained throughout the assignment, is necessary for obtaining additional assignments from the customer at the conclusion of a project, and should continue even after your work for that client is finished. Since you are already familiar with the customer, you may be able to identify new problems you could solve in the future. Successful business and salespeople maintain periodic scheduled contact with all of their former clients to keep themselves in their clients' minds.

3 **Diplomacy**—networkers have little, if any, authority to make things happen. You must rely on your ability to persuade people to take action. Former business executives from large companies who become entrepreneurs often have difficulty making the transition from a decision maker to one who influences others to take action.

THE TRAITS OF SUCCESSFUL NETWORKERS

4   **Communication skills**—you may possess all nine of the other skills listed, but if you can't communicate effectively, your career in business will be very short-lived. Rapport and understanding among you, your networkers and your customers is the basis for the "chemistry" which must exist if the project or sale is going to be truly successful from the customer's point of view. Without good communication skills, you will not be able to develop a network, sell a proposal, gather accurate data from interviews, or have your ideas accepted.

At the top of the list among communication skills are sharp listening skills. Being able to draw information during an interview will greatly influence how a problem is perceived. Customers tend to judge you on your willingness to listen to them. It is an all too common mistake to try to dazzle customers with the breadth of your knowledge by talking too much. An adage we often use with our clients is, "Remember, we were created with two ears and one mouth—they should be used proportionately."

Cogent writing ability is the means by which you demonstrate that you have listened to and understand the needs of the customer. If your letters, marketing materials or proposals are not clear and to the point, or contain typos or misspelled words, your chances of winning a client are nil.

Oral presentation skills are also vital. It is not enough to know the answers to the customer's needs; you must be able to clearly respond to them. A single poorly phrased response can cast a shadow over your credibility.

SUCCESSFUL BUSINESS NETWORKING

5 **Flexibility**—no two members of your network and no two customers are exactly the same; in fact, they may differ widely. Even if you work in a particular industry, the culture of different people and organizations within that industry will likely test your ability to adapt. Dress codes, levels of formality and informality, decision-making processes, and the personalities of the people you have to deal with will be different. An ability to adapt and fit in is very helpful to gain trust. Sticking out like a sore thumb does not engender openness on the part of your networkers or your customers.

6 **Diagnostic and problem-solving skills**—good businesspeople and successful networkers are problem finders as well as problem solvers. Rarely will customers accurately identify their problems or needs. More than likely you will have to ferret out the underlying issues. It helps to be curious by nature; even being nosy can be a positive attribute that helps you avoid superficial or simplistic explanations which lead to improper referrals.

7 **Self-discipline**—successful networkers and businesspeople are generally very bright people. Yet it is the customer who is the "boss"—even if the customer is not as well-educated or as sophisticated as you are. It takes a good deal of self-discipline to remember this. You must also discipline yourself to take care of yourself emotionally and physically. Without preventive self care, it is even easy for highly successful networkers to burn out.

8 **Resourcefulness**—if solutions to problems were readily available, your customer would find the answer without your help. Customers expect those referred to them to be ahead of the curve when it comes to knowledge of their field of expertise,

THE TRAITS OF SUCCESSFUL NETWORKERS

and to be able to locate and access hard to get materials. Your customers will expect you to be informed and articulate about the latest techniques and theories in your field. You may not know all of the answers to all of the questions, but you will be expected to find or develop answers to most of them.

9 **Self-confidence**—as a networker on either the giving or receiving end of a referral, when things go wrong during a project—and they will, you will be blamed; when things go right, the customer takes the credit. If you must have center stage and rely on the recognition of others to stroke your ego, you will not go far as a networker. Successful networkers derive satisfaction from knowing that they are good at what they do. At times you may be called upon to defend the strength of your convictions by telling a member of your network, and even customers, what they need to hear even when they do not want to.

When giving referrals, however, most of the time you will be working backstage; and even when the project is a huge success, it is unlikely that the customer will say "thank you" or even acknowledge your contributions. Most good networkers are highly altruistic and enjoy knowing that they have helped clients succeed, even if they do not receive accolades for having done so.

Successful networkers must be self-confident, self-motivated, self-fulfilled, and practitioners of the power of positive thinking. For successful networkers, every challenge is a new opportunity, and every failure represents a learning experience.

10 **Creative time management**—in addition to everything else, you must be able to juggle numerous, often conflicting, demands for

your time and attention. It is rare for businesspeople who are successful networkers to be able to focus solely on one relationship or one customer for any considerable length of time. And even if you are able to devote yourself to only one customer or project, or to the needs of your network, you must still find time to market. On top of this, you may have a family which expects some of your time, as well as the need to continue your professional development, the desire to be involved in community or parental programs, and, if you can swing it, maybe you can devote some time to socializing or personal growth. Successful networkers learn to manage their time effectively.

ADDITIONAL TRAITS OF SUPERIOR NETWORKERS

Successful networkers have learned to master the ten traits listed above. Superior networkers have also developed another set of skills which enables them to rise to the top. These additional characteristics include:

- **Relationship building**—the best networkers can cultivate and manage relationships. They do everything they can to gain the trust and confidence of their clients and the members of their networks. Their focus is on the long-term relationship, not just the short-term project. They will walk the extra mile to keep customers happy and exceed people's expectations.

- **Management ability and group dynamics skills**—we have often described running a network as akin to trying to herd cats.

THE TRAITS OF SUCCESSFUL NETWORKERS 137

Because they are bright, creative, self-confident and able to work without direct supervision, the members of your network can be notoriously independent. Yet teamwork is essential when a diverse group of talented people are brought together to work as a functioning network. Without skilled leadership, the effort could soon result in chaos. Successful networks do not happen by accident. They are the result of good project management and group dynamic techniques.

○ **Organizational awareness**—the best networkers are able to keep the big picture in sight. They can envision and help clients to understand their organization as a system and see how a problem—or even the solution to a problem in one area—will impact other parts or departments of the company. They can see interrelationships and can avoid "the operation was a success, but the patient died" type of error. They are also very good at identifying additional opportunities in which other members of their network can be of service to the client, because they help the client to recognize other problems which need to be solved.

○ **Ability to develop others**—training and mentoring the members of your network are critical to your future. Yet far too few experienced businesspeople are willing to devote the time necessary to nurture and develop their networkers. The true professionals in the world of networking recognize and accept the need to share their "secrets" with those whom they will give referrals and those from whom they will receive referrals.

BE A SILLY GOOSE

When I was a kid and would do something funny or silly, my grand-mother would usually tell me to "stop being a silly goose." So naturally I grew up thinking geese were somehow silly creatures. But recently I learned some pretty interesting things about geese that show they aren't so silly after all. In fact, some of their actions prove that geese are actually downright smart and that we can all learn some effective networking concepts from them. For example:

○ Each of the birds in the flock helps to lift and support the other members of the flock. By flying in their famous "V" formation, each bird creates an updraft for the bird behind it. In this forma-tion, the flock faces less wind resistance and, together, they can fly more than 70 percent farther than a single bird flying alone.

You can choose to "fly solo" if you wish and try to do everything for yourself, but you can be sure that your savviest competitors will instead be forming relationships and coalitions to compete against you. In today's competitive business market you need all the help you can get. You have more thrust when you pool your efforts with a group of people who want to help you because you will be helping them.

○ Whenever a goose decides to drop out of formation and strike out on its own, it suddenly experiences the drag and effort of trying to fly without the lifting power of the other members of the group. It doesn't take long for the goose to return to the "V" formation to be "lifted up" by the rest of the group.

THE TRAITS OF SUCCESSFUL NETWORKERS

Successful networkers have learned that not only can they go father with the assistance of others, but that it is also more fun to have other people to bounce ideas off of who can boost them up when things get tough. They have also learned that they do not always need to blaze new trails. Sometimes the tried and true ways of doing things really do work best: following the leader is not always a bad thing.

○ When the lead goose in the formation gets tired, it moves back into the flock, and another goose takes over the lead. The goose at the head of the formation has no air current to ride on like the rest of the flock does. The lead goose establishes the airflow and the lift for those who come behind. It is hard work and requires time off.

People are the same way. Successful networkers, like successful leaders, realize that they can accomplish much more by sharing the workload. If they don't, the entire team will suffer. All of the members of your network work interdependently with you and with each other. You should not feel that you have to be in charge of everything. You want to be in touch with what is going on within your network and among the members, but you don't always have to be in control.

○ The geese in the formation honk from behind to encourage those up front to keep up their speed.

Everybody needs to receive words of encouragement to sustain them. Unfortunately, far too few people are willing to give them. Most people spend time telling one another what they are doing wrong—"You know that referral that you gave me last week?

Well you sure missed to boat on that one"—rather than on encouraging them to keep up the good work they are doing. Just because it's a truism doesn't mean it's not true: people really do respond better to praise than to criticism. Besides, you will certainly attract more people into your network if they think of you as a nice person rather than a grouch.

○ Should a member of a flock become ill, or get wounded or shot down, two other geese drop out of formation and follow their comrade down to help and protect it. They stay with the weak goose until it is able to fly again or dies. Then they set out again and join another formation or catch up with their original flock.

It's easy to stick together when everything is going right and to ride along on the good work of another. But when things go wrong, some people take the opportunity to criticize or blame those they once honored.

NOTE

Remember these lessons from the "silly" geese when dealing with those in your network. Be ready to help those who have fallen on hard times. Be willing to go even farther out of your way to assist those who are less fortunate than yourself. Be known as a person who fulfills commitments, and others will be more likely to be committed to you.

Chapter 10

DEVELOPING YOUR NETWORKING SKILLS

NETWORKING IS NOT A FULL TIME JOB— IT'S A WAY OF LIFE

The first thing you must know is that networking is not a God-given gift; it is a skill. If you know people who seem to be natural networkers, it is not because they were born that way. It is a byproduct of their personality development. Although the ability to network may seem innate, it was actually developed through many years in their family culture.

Remember that relationship building in friendships and relationship building in business are two very different animals. You must practice business networking skills until they become habits. You cannot network only part time. It is not something you turn on or turn off. You must believe in the process.

You must have the mind set that anytime you can build a relationship with anyone, you will. Anytime you can help someone in their business or personal life, you will do it. Truly effective and successful networkers love to help others. Networking for them is not something they do, it is a way of life. They have a sharing mentality.

This system is about how to increase your business success through networking. When you network, you have a self-serving reason for doing so. There is nothing wrong with that as long as you help others before they help you. Don't just call someone out of the blue and expect them to perform for you. Relationships take time, and each of your Networking Associates must see and feel your sincerity. If you want something from someone, you must first give it. If you do not give, then you have no justification for getting upset when you do not receive.

EDUCATE, TRAIN AND NURTURE YOUR SALES FORCE

The first step in building an effective team of Networking Associates is building quality relationships. The second is education. You must educate your associates about yourself and your business. This is a never-ending process. To help your associates understand, it is important to break things down and make them as simple as possible.

DEVELOPING YOUR NETWORKING SKILLS

I'm sure we have all heard that when advertising, you should gear your advertisement to the mind of a ten-year-old. Is that because we think people are stupid? Actually, it's quite the opposite. Because we know how smart people are and how professional they are at what they do, they are very focused on specific goals in their personal and business lives. The only way for you to get them to understand what you do is to make it so simple that they can't forget, especially when you are first establishing a relationship.

At the onset of the relationship, your associates may not quite understand why this relationship with you is important to them. As time goes by and they see what you have been doing for them, they will want to do more for you. At that time they will pay more attention to what you tell them. Until then, remember that only after a person sees or hears an advertisement at least seven times do they actually act on it. Repetition is the key. If you can get them to remember what you do, you have hurdled the first step, and it's a big one.

Here is a list of what you need to tell your associates about yourself:

1. Years of experience
2. Training, certification
3. Professional associations
4. Personal corporate philosophy
5. Competitive advantage
6. Uniqueness
7. Passion: Why you do what you do
8. When you work

9 Work ethic and values

10 Past successes

11 Customer problems and how you resolved them

12 Mistakes and how you've corrected them

13 Guarantees

14 Your goals for your business

15 Lifestyle goals

16 The job you made no money on

17 The greatest length you've gone to for a customer

18 How what you are doing will enhance other lives

19 Who is your ideal customer

20 What are some of the signs to look for that say someone needs your service

21 Good information to know about

22 Good contacts or connections

23 Referral policy

24 Specials, discounts, etc.

25 Catchphrase

1. Years of experience—it is important to let your associates know how many years of experience you have in your profession and how long it took to become a professional in that field. For instance, a 33-year-old thoracic surgeon has spent one year as a full time surgeon, but she also has four years of college, four years of medical school, three years of internship and three years as a surgical resident—nevermind the hundreds of hours of continuous education in the field on a yearly basis.

A plumber has to be an apprentice plumber for seven years before he is licensed in New York State. You may be licensed for only two years yet have nine years of experience. What if your family was in the same business as you are? If your dad was a plumber and you have helped him since you were 10 years old, I bet you have more experience than the guy two years out of college who decided he wanted to be a plumber and had never done it before. If your family owns a real estate agency, an insurance agency, a restaurant, or a financial planning firm, this all adds to your years of experience.

How long have you been doing what you're doing and in what different capacities? If you told me you went to college for engineering and then, after graduating, you had to work at the family restaurant because your dad was sick; as opposed to telling me that you started working in the restaurant cleaning dishes when you were 14 and moved up from bus boy, to waiter, to bartender, to assistant manager, to manager, before becoming the owner, I will see that you know this business from the inside out and that you know what it takes to make it successful at every level. Don't sell yourself short. Let people know your true experience in the business.

2. Training, Certification—what type of training did you have to go through to get to where you are? Did you have to get certified, and if so, what did it take to get that certification? If you're a certified public accountant (CPA), you want people to know what that means. You probably think everyone knows. You're wrong. Most people don't.

You have to assume that nobody knows about you, your profession, its training, etc. Most people know that if you are a CPA, that means you are an accountant. But they have no idea what it took for you to become a CPA. You need to let them know that. Why? Because it is impressive and lets your associates know how committed you are to your profession and becoming the best that you can be. Do people know that besides four years of college majoring in accounting (which is torture enough in my opinion), after you graduate you have to take a two-day test for eight hours each day to get your certification. (No thanks!) Then you have to audit at an accounting firm for two years and 80 hours of continuing education are required every two years to maintain your certification. Believe me, that's impressive. Whatever your profession, determine how much training was necessary before you were considered a professional.

3. Professional associations—this is more important than you know. It's important that you are involved in professional associations in your field because they are educational and informational networks. It is also important that your associate knows you are involved because it shows your level of commitment to your given profession and lets them know that you are up to date on the latest things happening in your industry. You are continuing your education on a regular basis. An associate of mine told me that the electrician union he belongs to requires him to take 20 hours of continuing education per year. This keeps him up on the latest electrical codes and safety findings. I didn't even know that this existed. But now that I do, I'm impressed. I like the fact that the people in my network are always pushing to make themselves better. That's what I do, and that is a quality I want in the people I associate with.

DEVELOPING YOUR NETWORKING SKILLS

4. Personal corporate philosophy—does your company have a corporate philosophy or a mission statement? If not, you need to develop one. If you own your own business, you need to develop one for your company and then you need to have your employees or associates do the same for their division of the company and for themselves personally. If you work for a company or you are an independent sales representative, you need to develop one for yourself. Your personal mission statement tells who you are as a business and what you are all about. It is the generalization of your values.

I know what you're thinking. Why do I need this? It's just more work and time spent doing something that no one will ever see but me. You need to do this to make it clear in your mind what your real mission is. If you can't write it down on paper very precisely, then you can't communicate it well to others even if you think you can. The other advantage of writing it down is that you are going to give a copy of it to your Networking Associates. You want them to know what your mission is and how strongly you believe in it. The fact that you're even bringing it up in conversation will impress them enough. To actually have it written out and hand it to them shows them your conviction, as well as organization, about your business. They will probably ask you how you came up with it and if you could help them write one of their own. Nobody likes to feel that they are missing out. By helping them develop their own mission statement, you will have done another favor for them and shown another professional side of yourself. Will this translate into monetary gains from referrals—you better believe it.

5. Competitive advantage—what is it that gives you a competitive advantage over your competitor? A friend of mine who owns a martial arts school told me that every school in the association he is involved in sells annual contracts to its members and has a direct funds withdrawal set up with their bank accounts. These schools offer a one-time 15-minute introductory lesson for $9.95. In contrast, he developed the competitive advantage of not offering annual memberships. All of his memberships are three-month sessions, and he offers a free two-week trial membership. For first-time members he offers an eight-week introductory session at a discount. These unique options give him a competitive advantage. He gets a lot of calls and has increased his membership dramatically. If you currently don't have a competitive advantage, get one. Look at what your competitors are doing and see what you can do differently to cause your potential clients to call you before them. Everyone wants a bargain, so if you design one, make sure your Networking Associates know about it because they would love to brag about a person they know with the best deal in town. It makes them look better.

6. **Uniqueness**—what is it that makes you unique? It can be anything: the multiple generations your family has been in the business, the hunger you have to be successful, your philosophy, your training, some of the equipment you have that no one else in the area has, how clean you keep your trucks, how often you keep in contact with your clients, your newsletter, articles that have been written about you, articles that you have written. Do you get the idea? Sit down and list your unique features and the unique benefits your clients get from working with you. Uniqueness is a great selling point for you and for your associates. It gives them something to brag about. "My accountant Steve, he is so disciplined. Not only is he the best accountant, but he finished a 26-mile marathon in less than 3½ hours, and that was during tax season." Does this have anything to do with his accounting

DEVELOPING YOUR NETWORKING SKILLS

149

ability? Not directly. But it does tell you something about the person, and it gives you a reason to brag about the quality of people you are associated with. There are over six billion people on earth, and there is not one who is exactly like you. Let your associates know why.

7. Passion: Why you do what you do—do you have a passion for what you do? I hope so. I like to associate with businesspeople who are passionate about their profession. To me this means they see the bigger picture above and beyond money. They love the technical, creative and challenging aspects of their business. They are always trying to improve their knowledge, ability, efficiency, productivity and therefore, their bottom line. They understand that making money is a natural byproduct of doing your job with passion. They have the passion to be the best. They desire to push themselves to become the best that they can be. If you're the best, the money will come. If people see your passion and your sincerity in your professional purpose, you will have more work than you can handle through word of mouth. Make sure your associates know of your passion and know how deep it runs. They will admire and respect you for it, and it will probably rub off on them. Everyone needs that passionate motivation every now and then. You could be their source, and down the road they can be yours.

8. When you work—do you have specific hours that you work? Is it nine to five? Do you have a 24-hour service call? Weekends? Weeknights? It is important for your associates to know when you work, especially if your hours set you apart from your competition. Make sure they know so they can qualify a potential client. Instead of getting a referral that does not work out because of a specific need for certain hours, your associate has let them know your availability ahead of time. The better educated I am, the better I can sell you.

9. Work ethic and values—when I was in high school my parents had our downstairs hallway redone. This consisted of ripping off all the old wallpaper, rehanging new paper and then painting all the trim. It wasn't the biggest job, but it definitely paid some bills for the painters. One day my mother and I walked in at around 5:30 P.M., and they had already finished for the day. That itself was not the problem. The problem was that they left the hallway, which we used every day to go in and out of the garage, as it was. It appeared that at 5:00 P.M. they stopped whatever they were doing and just walked out. The place was a mess and we could hardly walk through it. My mother couldn't believe they left our home like this and I said, naively, "They must have gone out for something, no one would leave someone else's house like this." I was wrong.

What does this tell you about their work ethic and their values? A person with a good work ethic approximates where they will be at "quitting" time and finishes the job that is in the works before they actually call it a day—even if it is after the estimated work day. This shows that their ethics are based on quality workmanship, not on the time clock. A person with good work values treats others people's property as their own, or better than their own. Would you leave a person's house in total disarray? I remember a saying a friend of mine in the television production industry once told me, "Take only pictures, leave no footprints." I have applied that to everything I do. All the people I associate with believe this. Could you imagine referring a contractor to friend's home and receiving a complaint that things were missing or the place was left a mess or damaged? Yikes! Let your Networking Associates know in no uncertain terms your high work ethic and values. It will go a long way in their referring you. By the way, the people mentioned above who worked on our hallway put my

DEVELOPING YOUR NETWORKING SKILLS

parents down as a recommendation. The people that called my parents for a reference ended up not hiring them... are you surprised?

10. Past successes—your past success stories with your clients are a very important part of who you are. If you could have some of your clients write letters of recommendation about you and the success you had with them, that would be a great marketing tool. Don't be afraid; if you ask one of your clients to write a letter, suggest that you could write the letter for them, and if they agreed with what you wrote they could sign it. Many people would love to help you but don't like to write or consider it a major hassle. They will be relieved if you offer to do it for them. If you have some of these letters, they would be a great thing to share with your Networking Associates. If you don't have any letters, then just share some success stories.

One of my associates shared a story with me about a couple he went to see. The gentleman was a few years from retirement and had a few good long-term investments. After taking a look at their portfolio, my associate said that one of the things they needed was a good life insurance policy. He explained that if one of them died, the other would be left with all the current bills. Even though they had a pretty good nest egg now, it would dwindle away very quickly if they had only one income. They weren't sure what to do, and he got them some good insurance. Two years later the husband died and the wife was very worried about expenses. When she realized that the insurance she was receiving was going to be more than enough, she called my friend and thanked him for his concern and intelligent insight into their future. She said that because of him she had nothing to worry about financially for the remainder of her life. That's a pretty nice story. He told me, "That's what I do. I insure people's financial future and it makes me feel great." Yes, I've referred him to many people I know. What are some of your success stories? Big or small, you've got to have them. Use them to let your associates know who you are and what you are all about.

11. Customer problems and how you resolved them—I believe that a person's professionalism is truly shown when they resolve a customer problem. Anyone can look and be professional when things are going well. It is when times get tough and the pressure is on that a person's true professional character emerges. Places like L.L. Bean and Talbots impress the heck out of me. They will take anything back at any time with no hassles and no questions. Customers walking into those stores have confidence. Knowing that whatever they buy can be returned at any time creates loyalty, and repeat business is second to none. I have never met a dissatisfied customer from either of the above companies. Never. That's amazing. I guess if you think about it, it's not really amazing. Their policies state that if the customer has a problem, they will solve it. How could you be dissatisfied with that? What are some of your customer relations policies or stories? As a Networking Associate I want to know. They add even greater credibility to who you are.

12. Mistakes and how you've corrected them—this is similar to customer problems, but the main difference is that you actually made a mistake, big or small. When you realize that you have made a mistake, what do you do to rectify the situation? I know a contractor that also works as a handyman. He promised a lady that he would be at her house on a certain day at 1 P.M. to fix her sink. Well, he got tied up that day and couldn't get to her house. He called her when he arrived home and apologized. She was very upset and said that she

DEVELOPING YOUR NETWORKING SKILLS

had rearranged her whole day to accommodate his schedule. He said he understood and that he would make it up to her. He told her to make a list of all the little things she needed done in her house, and he promised her that besides fixing her sink the next day, he would give her three hours of his time—free of charge—to do anything she needed. She couldn't believe it. By the time he left the next day, not only did she forget that he had been late the previous day, but she offered him money for all the work he did in those three hours. He did not accept the money and just said her future business and recommendations to others was enough thanks for him. Guess who became his raving fan?

13. Guarantees—do you offer guarantees on your work or your products? If you do, that will make a *big* difference in the amount of business I could refer to you. People love to feel safe and secure. That's what a guarantee is, a big security blanket over their money. People work very hard for their money, and most don't mind spending it if they feel they are getting value for their dollar. A guarantee lets them know that not only did they buy a good product or service from you, but they also received an insurance policy on their purchase for free. You can't beat that peace of mind or that word of mouth. If you have a guarantee or when you do have one, put it in writing. This shows that you mean what you say. The guarantee is only as good as the person or company behind it. If it is in writing, then the person or company already has a greater perceived value. If you show me, "Satisfaction Guaranteed," I have nothing to lose.

14. Goals for your business—if you are a real estate agent and your goal is to become the number one salesperson in your area in the next two years and then open your own agency in the next five years, you should tell the people in your network. This shows commitment, planning, focus and professionalism. If your Networking Associates know you are going to be a significant player in your arena in the future, they will want to help you get there any way they can. Your success becomes their success. It will make them look good to know someone who is so well respected and successful, and they will want you as a part of their network. An influential person they know is in their circle.

15. Lifestyle goals—what type of future do you want for yourself and your family—a new home, specific cars, college for your children, retirement? Do you want to make money now so you can spend more time helping those who are less fortunate? The more specific your goals are for both your business and your life, the more likely that they will actually happen. If you have specific goals and plan and schedule time to achieve them, your goals will also appear more realistic to others. By telling your associates about your future lifestyle plans, you are bringing them into your personal life. This makes you a little more vulnerable but also more real and closer to them. They feel you have confided in them, and this makes them feel special. If they believe in you and what you stand for, then they will believe that you will achieve these goals and will want to be there to support you.

16. The job you made no money on—we all have a few of these—some of them without a choice. Out of the jobs that you made no money on or even lost money on, why did you do it or why did it happen? Were you satisfying a customer or trying to establish yourself? Did you realize that you made a mistake pricing the job halfway through but didn't want the customer to have to pay for your mistake? Everyone has a good story like this that usually exposes their character. Pick one, and let your associates know about it.

17. The greatest length you've gone to for a customer—have you ever gone above and beyond the call of duty for a customer? Have you done something that was not only unexpected but almost unbelievable? This is the best type of story to let people know about. A travel agent I am associated with received a phone call at 4 A.M. from clients who were supposed to go on their honeymoon to Bermuda later that day. Well, they woke up and saw the weather report and learned that there was a hurricane in Bermuda; and horrible weather was forecasted for the duration of their trip. The travel agent got out of bed, went to her office and logged on to the computer. To make a long story short, within 90 minutes she had them going to a new destination in the Cayman Islands for the same price; the agent paid the $50.00 cancellation fee as a wedding present. Wow, was I impressed. Anyone need to book a honeymoon?

18. How will what you do enhance other lives?—isn't this what life is all about? How can we all contribute to enhancing other lives through the work we do? No matter what you do for a living effects lives in some way. How and what is the contribution that you are making? If you're a plumber, you could feel good about the fact that quality work from you means clean, safe sewage or septic lines that won't contaminate fresh water lines or pollute the environment. I heard a photographer say that he didn't take pictures but created lasting memories and immortal spirits of the people he photographed. I like that. I enjoy seeing that kind of passion in people. Find the life enhancement in what you do and share it.

19. Who is your ideal customer/client?—make sure your associates know what makes a client desirable to you. Create a list if necessary. I may believe in you and want to refer you, but if I don't know what a good client is, I may let your big fish slip right out of my fingers, or my net. If you want referrals from me, then tell me what a good one is—and keep telling me. Once is never enough.

20. What are some of the signs to look for that tell you someone is in need of your service?—even if you educate your associates on what a good referral is for you, they may still miss a lot of opportunities to recommend you because they don't know the signs to look for that someone needs you. The chiropractor in my network told me that if you know someone who complains about a lot of sinus headaches and eye aches, they might have a slight allergy, but it is very likely that they have a subluxation of their cervical vertebrae. He also informed me that short-term consistent treatment could relieve the problem without any medication. After he told me that, I wasn't just looking for people with back problems to recommend him to, but I started recognizing people with sinus headaches. I asked them about their headaches and then told them what he told me. I was able to have him contact them to discuss their problem directly. It was pretty exciting to recognize a need and offer a solution. I would never have been able to do this if he didn't educate me on the signs to look for. What are the signs that people may need your service even if they don't know it yet?

21. Good information to know about—the advantage of having a strong and vast network is that you can have a great number of eyes and ears out there working for you. If you let your networkers know that you are always looking for good information on certain topics, they can let you know of happenings that you may never have found out about on your own.

22. Good contacts or connections—let your associates know what a good contact would be for you. Even if they don't know someone very

DEVELOPING YOUR NETWORKING SKILLS

well, it may be worth it for them to give you the name of someone in a certain company or position for you to send a letter to or call upon. Any contacts or connections you can get from your network should be more than appreciated.

23. Referral policy—many people I know set up referral policies. Things like, "For each referral you make to me, I will give you a percentage off of your next purchase or visit." Some give a referral fee, like a commission. The people in your networking levels usually won't need this type encouragement; they understand the power of the mutually beneficial relationship you have with them. A financial advisor I know has a newsletter and mentions those people who have referred business to him in it every month. This recognition keeps the referrals coming.

24. Specials, discounts, etc.—at certain times of the year you may offer specials or discount programs. This is of major importance, so let your associates know about it. People love to tell others about a great sale or deal they got. If I can tell you about a great sale going on and you get to take advantage of it, then I know you will do the same for me when you hear of one.

25. Catchphrase—how do you spell relief? Why is it we all answer this question incorrectly? Do you really spell relief, R-O-L-A-I-D-S? Of course not, but what a great catchphrase. This Rolaids commercial was released 20 years ago, and the answer they want us to have is still in our minds. Do you have a great catchphrase for you and your business? If not, it is time to develop one that will keep you remembered even when you are not around. You never want to be out of sight and out of mind. To start, you need to think about and list the benefits your business gives to its clients. If you are a financial planner, you provide peace of mind about future financial security.

A dentist gives "healthy teeth," (that's OK), "beautiful teeth," (that's better), "an infectious smile," (hey not bad!).

Okay, once you've figured out your benefits, you have to think of what you are "selling" in your catchphrase. Are you selling yourself or your company? One is not better than the other, but I personally like it when your phrase is a personal reflection of you. If you own your own company, it shows your true commitment to your customers, and if you work for a large corporation or franchise, it gives you your own identity above and beyond the company. Remember that when people refer you for business, it is you they are referring, not your business.

Some examples:

- "At the Bank of New York Mortgage company we want to be the start of your dreams and the end of your nightmares."

- "If you want to travel near or far, Zeca travel is your star. Let us be your guiding light."

- "Cup of Ads lets you drink your way to profits."

- "If you're in need a of a new house, if you're smart you'll let Gloria do your homework."

What you want to stay away from are the big corporate identities like "Just do it." Even though you know this catchphrase represents Nike, the question is, how many millions of dollars did it cost them to create that corporate identity? Think about it. They have hired the top athletes in the world to endorse their product and have taken out many full-page ads in magazines and newspapers. They have produced elaborate television commercials, and they sponsor sporting event

DEVELOPING YOUR NETWORKING SKILLS 159

after sporting event. That's a lot of cash. So don't try to be cutesy with a catchphrase that doesn't identify what you do.

DON'T GET MIXED UP BY MIXERS

The biggest problem most people have with going to a mixer is that they really don't understand the purpose of it. The purpose is not to go and pass out as many business cards as you can to people, nor is it to get as many business cards as you can from people. In fact, unless it is stated otherwise, the point of a social mixer for any organization is to socialize. Most people think they are supposed to go there and do business. They're wrong. The point of a social event at an association, chamber or any other business group is to develop relationships, to meet new people and to get to know your current business acquaintances better. There is a business reason behind the social mixer, and that's why it is sponsored by a business group; but the purpose of the event itself is social.

However, there is a strategy you can follow to make these events work for you. You need to set goals when you go to these meetings so you leave not only happy that you had a nice social evening, but satisfied that it was also a productive use of your time. You have two main goals when attending any mixer:

1 To meet a certain number of new, potential associates for your network.

2 To develop deeper relationships with your current Networking Associates.

Before you go to a mixer, set a goal of how many new people you are going to meet that night to form a bond with. We recommend aiming for five to 10 percent of those attending. If you go to a mixer and there are 60 people in attendance, plan to meet and really talk to three to six new people. If you are at a mixer with 200 people, then 10 to 20 people is your range, although in our experience, meeting 20 new people at any one event is not likely to occur.

When we talk about meeting new people, we are not talking about getting their business cards. You want to find out about them. When you speak with them, ask questions about them and their business. Find a hobby, interest, sport or cause that you have in common. Let them know that you are looking to build your network of people you can refer business to and ask if they would like to get together in the next week or two. Get their business card, write some notes on it from your conversation and move on to someone else.

Remember to avoid hanging out with those people who you already know well at a mixer. If you have a strong Primary Networking relationship with someone, you don't need to spend time with them at the mixer. Say hello, let them know your goals for the evening, encourage them to do the same and be on your way.

Mixers that business organizations sponsor are meant for you to network with others, not to separate into groups like oil and water. I love it when I speak to someone who has gone to a mixer and they say, "I went last night but it was a joke. I didn't get any business out of it." I then ask what they did at the mixer. They give the usual response, "Just talked to a few of my friends the whole night." They didn't mingle. They didn't approach one other person, introduce themselves or pass out any business cards. They went to a mixer, but

DEVELOPING YOUR NETWORKING SKILLS **161**

they didn't mix. That makes as much sense as joining a health club, going three days a week to train, but instead just watching TV and drinking some of the nutritional products. Are you joining to actually work out or to say you're working out? Are you a member of the business organization to increase your business and meet others in the local business community, or are you a member to say you're a member? Is it worth it to pay a couple of hundred dollars a year just to be able to say you're a member? I take a more proactive approach. If I pay a couple of hundred dollars to be a member of an organization, it becomes my organization. This means that when I go to a mixer, I'm going to act like I'm the president by being polite and greeting all the other members. As I "mix," people begin to feel comfortable. You have to keep in mind that everyone in that room has the same concerns and fears that you do. That's why they are in little cliques and not mingling. Break the ice and you will be remembered, admired and respected.

NETWORKING TOOLS

There are seven main tools that will help you become an effective business networker at a mixer. They should be with you at all times:

1 Business cards

2 Name badge

3 Your marketing button

4 Personal referral card

5 Business card holder

6 Breath neutralizers

7 The Rule of "7s"

Business Cards

Not only do you need to have your business card on you at all times, but you need to have an effective business card. What do I mean by effective? I mean a card that has all the information I need to contact you and that tells me exactly what it is that you do. As basic as this seems, some of you might be surprised by some of the business cards I have received. Some of the cards I got from people didn't have their own name on it, or it didn't have the address, or the information was printed in such small type that I couldn't read it, or there was so much information on the card that I couldn't find the name, address or phone number easily. There is only one card I've seen that had just a personal name on it. George Burns handed it to John Denver in the movie, *Oh God*. Printed directly in the middle of that card was the name "GOD." George Burns, who played God, gave it to John Denver's character and said that if anyone needed proof that God had talked to him, he should just show them His card. It didn't work. So even if you're as well known as God, you should have at least the following items on your card:

1 Your company's name

2 Your name

3 Your position

4 Your phone number(s)

5 Your Fax number

DEVELOPING YOUR NETWORKING SKILLS

6   Your e-mail address (if you have one)

7   Your mailing address (landmark reference if necessary)

8   What your company does in five words or less

9   Your Photo

10 Your personal catchphrase

ABC COMPANY
3 Generations of Widget Manufacturing

Johnathan Smith
Sales Representative

"Your 100% satisfaction is my business."

125 Main Street
Anytown, NY 12345-6789   USA
www.abccomp.com

Phone 914-333-8888
Fax   914-333-8889
jsmith@abc.com

1. Your company's name—your company name identifies you. It is important to remember that even though your company name means a lot to you, nine times out of 10, it means very little to the person you hand your business card to. They are interested in developing a relationship with you, not just your company, or at least they should be. However, it is important that your company name is remembered and easily identified, so make sure the logo is printed clearly and prominently. Part of marketing your company is having a clear and consistent logo. No matter what your logo is printed on, it should always look the same.

2. Your name—this is the most important feature of any card. If I can't easily find your name, then the whole purpose of the card has been lost. You give someone your business card so they have a record of you. Make sure your name is the focus of the card and easily readable. One of the basic rules of sales is to take away all reasons to say no before they happen. If I can't easily find your name on your card, that alone could be enough reason to discard it.

3. Your position—I have too many cards that show a person's name and the company name, but I have no idea what the person does for the company. When you are networking at business mixers and you hand out cards, it is not likely everyone is going to remember you and what you do. Your card is a marketing tool and must be simple and straightforward. Underneath your name on your card, make sure you have clearly printed your position in your company.

4. Your phone numbers—the main reason I refer to a card is to contact you. If your phone number is not easy to find, it gives me a reason to get annoyed and call someone else. Your phone number should be in large type, not hidden in four point type on the back. Make your phone numbers easy to find on the front of your card, near your name and company. If you have a bi-fold card, make sure your pertinent information is on the front and everything else is in the interior. I don't want to flip back and forth from your name to the phone number. If you have multiple phone lines like business, home, voice mail and pager, make sure they are clearly marked and that the most important one is on top of the others, preferably in bold.

5. Your fax number—if you have multiple phone numbers and fax lines, it is best to keep your main phone line and fax together and then separate the others. So much communication today is done by

DEVELOPING YOUR NETWORKING SKILLS

fax that it is important that you make it easy to find. If you don't have a fax line, get one. You look less professional without it. To be a player you must keep up with technology in your business. A few years ago fax lines were optional. Today e-mail is optional and faxes are essential. Put down this book, go order a new phone line and buy a fax machine now. You won't regret it.

6. Your e-mail address—if you have one, put it on your card proudly. You are not only a businessperson of today, but you are moving your company into the twenty-first century. This is such a great way to communicate with people that you shouldn't let it pass you by. Your e-mail address should be directly below your fax line so I have your three main contact points easily accessible to me. When you do have an e-mail address, make it simple and straightforward. Try to stay away from cute names like the old CB handles we had when I was a kid. (Yes, I had a CB and my handle was Robin Hood—at least until someone else told me it was theirs!)

7. Your mailing address (landmark reference if necessary)—make sure your full address is on your card. This may be the only record someone has of you, and if your address is not on it in full, they will not be able to send you something that may be of value to you. If your mailing address is not the easiest to find, then put a brief landmark description next to the street address so it can be found by car (for example, one block off main street).

8. What your company does in five words or less—a five-word description of what your company does, if it is not blatantly obvious, may be imperative. For example, if your company is Smith and Associates and your title is Sales Consultant, I still don't know what you do. So, underneath Smith and Associates include, "Wholesale Paper Manufacturers" (or whatever your company does).

9. Your photo—if you have your photo on your card, people will remember you and keep your card around longer. If I file your card and don't speak with you for a while, I will forget about you. Out of sight, out of mind. People who market their products don't do it with words only. Photos grab attention and create an instant relationship. You can personalize who you are by having your photo on your card. If it doesn't go against your professional image, invest in quality photo business cards.

10. Your personal catchphrase—this gives me part of you. It makes the card more personal and reminds me of what you are all about: "The dentist that gives you a million dollar smile"; "Honesty is my best policy."

Remember that your card is a marketing tool. It gives people the information they need about you at their fingertips, and it reminds them who you are and what you are all about when you are not around. Don't make your card a book. I have seen cards with double folds, which are not bad; but if you list everything in the world that your company does as well as include a proverbial story that is by no means brief, nobody will read or care about it. Make your card short, to the point and easy to read. It's good to be creative, but don't let creativity override effectiveness.

Your card is a networking tool, and, therefore, a marketing tool. The key to effective marketing is simplicity in a message that won't be forgotten. No matter what size company you work for, look at the business cards and make sure they are achieving their purpose. Don't get stuck thinking, "...that's the way everyone else's card is." This simple tool is so often designed incorrectly and ineffectively. This is one of your foundations of networking that helps build your business; so make it a strong one.

Name Badge

Whenever you go to a business mixer or social event, it is important to wear a name badge. The name badge makes you stand out in the crowd. I'm not talking about those stick on name badges that say, "Hello, my name is...," although if you have nothing else, these will be adequate for the day. You should create your own personal name badge that very clearly states your name and your company. At your local business supply store you can pick up a name badge holder. You can then create your own name badge that reflects your personal image. It can be fun, conservative, rich looking or whatever you want. The idea is to draw attention to yourself so people will want to speak with you. On the next page are some good examples of name badges that are creative yet informative.

Your Marketing Button

Your marketing button is a regular pin-on button, about two inches in diameter, that has your own saying on it. If you are looking to build your network you might want to include an appropriate phrase: "Would you like a referral for your business?"; "Have I given you business yet?"; "Are you in my Primary Network?"; "Are you Primary, Secondary, Dormant or Inactive?" The idea is to get people interested in what the button says and to ask you about it. When you explain to them what it means, you have created an opening to make them part of your network. Look below for a variety of marketing button catchphrases, or make up your own.

Marketing Button Catchphrases:

- Would you like a referral for your business?
- Have I given you business yet?
- Do you want pre-qualified customers?
- Interested in free advertising?

DEVELOPING YOUR NETWORKING SKILLS

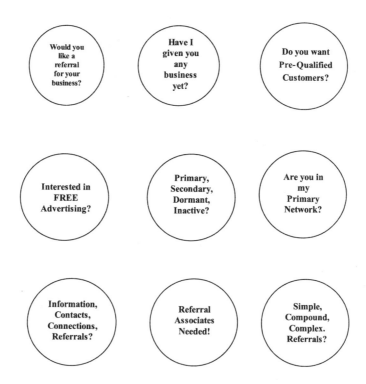

- Are you Primary, Secondary, Dormant or Inactive?
- Are you in my Primary Network?
- Do you need information, contacts, connections or referrals?
- Referral associates needed!
- Are you getting Simple, Compound or Complex Referrals?
- Build your business through word of mouth.

Personal Referral Card

A Personal Referral Card is the size of a business card that you should carry with you so you can refer anyone in your network to anyone else at any time. Most of us are not able to carry around all of our networkers'

SUCCESSFUL BUSINESS NETWORKING

business cards, but if you usually carry the Networker's Address Book containing this information, you could easily connect someone with a person in your network.

Use the card on the next page as a template for your own Personal Referral Card. Make a card with your information on the top and bottom, and have a printer make up 500 or so for you. Keep a bunch of these with you in your wallet, organizer, business card holder, jacket pocket, etc. When you find a person with a need you can help with, take out the card, get your associate's information and fill in your Personal Referral Card. This makes you look well organized, as well as committed to and confident in your networkers. This card shows how serious you are about helping your associates, and it should commit them to you at the same level. If you have the Successful Business Networker's Organizer or Computer Disk program, you can get this information right from your Networking Associates Address Book.

To make your card complete, give the following information:

1 Associate's name

2 Profession

3 Company

4 Phone

5 Fax

6 E-mail

Remember, even though you are giving out this referral today, the person you are giving the referral to may not call for a few days. That

DEVELOPING YOUR NETWORKING SKILLS

171

is why they need this information: so they don't forget who it was or what it was for.

> **A PERSONAL REFERRAL FROM**
> **THE NETWORK OF FRANK J. DE RAFFELE JR.**
>
> Name:_____
> Profession:_____
> Company:_____
> Phone:_____
> Fax:_____
> E-mail:_____
> Note:_____
>
> Phone: 914-838-2805 Fax: 914-838-1531 E-Mail: fderaffele@aol.com

Breath Neutralizers

Networking is a person to person activity. If you are going to be speaking with people face to face you don't want to offend them with your breath. At all times you should carry some type of breath neutralizer.

I was speaking with a gentleman at a business function a few months back and I couldn't wait to get away from him. The first strike against him was that he was a close talker. You know, one of those guys who stands about six to eight inches from you when he talks. He could have had the breath of rose petals and would have still bothered me. The problem was he didn't. Not only was he invading my personal space (12 to 18 inches) but his breath was literally making me gag. I didn't hear or listen to one word he said. To this day, I don't remember his name, profession or even which business organization meeting I was at. But I do remember him. That face is branded in my memory. I will never let him corner me again. And yes, it was at this time that I started carrying a breath neutralizer. I don't ever want to offend someone like that. Choose your favorite: gum, mints, breath spray or a can of Lysol if necessary, but choose something and don't leave home without it.

The Rule of "7s"

Think back to the last time you met someone new. How long did it take you to form an opinion of that person? First impressions are a funny thing. If you see me well before meeting me, you will form your first impression on my physical appearance alone. Once we have met, I have to overcome it or live up to it, depending on whether your first impression was positive or negative. Besides being conscious of our physical appearance through exercise, eating habits, the clothes we wear and how we groom ourselves, there is not much else we can do to affect a person's impression of us until we actually meet them and have a conversation.

Once you begin a conversation you have 7 seconds to make a first impression, 14 seconds to create sufficient interest, and 21 seconds to tell your story. If you make it this far, you're in. This is known as the Rule of 7s. Each of these 7-second intervals is crucial for you in building a new relationship or reestablishing an old one.

In the first seven seconds you speak to someone, they are taking a lot in at once and are forming a quick opinion of you. They're basing their opinion on the pitch of your voice, its variation in tone, the speed at which you speak, the words that you use, the spirit you put in your conversation (are you sincerely interested in this conversation or do you seem like you want to be somewhere else), your eye contact or lack thereof, your hand gestures and general body language, your body and breath odor and your handshake, if applicable.

DEVELOPING YOUR NETWORKING SKILLS

That's a lot to absorb and form an opinion on in seven seconds. However, this is what happens. No one consciously processes all this information. With all of your senses at work, it only takes a few seconds before you are aware of movement, odors, physical contact and the sound of a voice. A second or two later, the brain processes what it thinks of all this sensory input.

If in these first few seconds you don't form a good first impression, you have a heck of a hole to dig yourself out of. When meeting people in business, your first impression is everything. If in those first few seconds I am not impressed with you, I may continue hearing you but I am no longer listening or interested in what you are saying.

The second seven-second interval is for creating interest. If you impressed someone during the first seven seconds, you have their attention. They are now looking for a "Why?"

- Why do they need to listen to you further?
- Why do they need to know more about your product or service?
- Why do they need to continue a relationship with you?

Previously we mentioned the difference between features and benefits. Remember? A feature is technical; a benefit is emotional. You want to let the person know the benefits you have to offer. Don't try to blatantly sell yourself. Rather, educate and inform them about yourself with sincerity. If you try to sell the "Whys," your selling will overshadow your sincerity. Besides, you are not trying to sell this person; you are trying to begin a relationship that can be developed over time that will be mutually beneficial to both of you. If you know your product or service well, all you need to do is quickly outline the benefits of it. This will let them create a small emotional attachment to it and you. This emotional attachment will create the motivation for them to ask "How?" If you can satisfy the whys, you will have opened the door for the next seven-second segment to answer the "How?" They now want to know more:

- ○ How will you, your product and service benefit them?
- ○ How does it (the product or service program) work?
- ○ How do they take advantage of it?

Your story should fulfill the "How?" or at least leave them wanting more. What you are trying to do is get them to want to speak with you further.

There are three sales you have to make here. First sell yourself to the person in the first seven seconds so they will be interested in listening to you for the next seven seconds. The second sale is creating a strong enough interest so they want to hear your story. The third is to tell your story in such a way that they will want to continue the conversation right then or at another time. If you can create this level of interest, then you are on your way to building a successful business relationship. The key is not to start speaking to someone with the idea of making the third sale before making the two sales preceding it. You will never start a relationship if you don't create a good impression and stimulate interest first.

DEVELOPING YOUR NETWORKING SKILLS

DIFFERENT TYPES OF NETWORKING (MARKETING)

There are three main types of networking that can sell your business to the public that cost you virtually nothing:

1   **Word-of-mouth**—this is what we are focusing on when we speak of building your networks and moving people up to your Primary Network so they will refer you to others and defend your honor whenever possible or necessary. For years all successful businesspeople have known that the most powerful form of advertising comes from the ground up. The grass roots approach—I tell two friends, and they tell two friends, etc.—is the way a business will be made or broken. I have seen multi-million-dollar companies with massive advertising campaigns fall to their knees because the word on the street was that the product or service was below adequate. Nothing can kill business quicker than bad word of mouth.

    However, up until recently no one has ever really designed a successful definitive way to market your business through word of mouth. By developing a strong network of people that you can build strong relationships with, you are embracing the foundation for any successful business or endeavor. By taking this proactive course, the only way your business can fail is if you don't live up to your promises.

2   **Public relations**—the kind of public relations we are talking about here is spreading positive word of mouth to a large number of people through direct or indirect informative marketing. These include: Press Releases, Articles, Sponsorship.

PRESS RELEASE

If you are not sending out press releases on a regular basis to your local newspapers, magazines, radio or TV stations, then you should start immediately. You are probably thinking, "What do I have to write a press release about?" More than you know. You must be creative. For example, let's say you're a chiropractor. You could send an informative press release containing some recent findings related to chiropractors and headaches, health, the immune system, or whatever timely information comes across your desk from your professional journals. People are always interested in preventive health issues. Local newspapers may be more than happy to run an article on a new finding in the health care industry that you may know about and they do not. No matter what size publication your press release goes in, it will be helpful. Not only will people see it, but you can clip the article and put it in your portfolio. It makes you a local celebrity, and everyone wants to do business with someone who is considered skilled at what they do.

How do you write one? The best way to practice is to get a local newspaper and read the articles and notice how all the major information is put in the first paragraph. This loading-up style of writing assumes that the reader is only going to read the first paragraph or two, and then move on to something else. This is how you have to write. Get all the important information in the first paragraph or two, and then leave the details for later paragraphs. If you hook the reader up front, they will want to read the rest of your story. If they get bored right away, they'll move on to something else.

FOR IMMEDIATE RELEASE

Contact: Joan Smith (888) 888-8888

New Book Is a Runaway Bestseller

Ut wisi enim ad min im veniam, quis nostrud exerci tation. Ullam corper suscipit lobortis nisl ut aliq uip ex ea commodo consequat. Lorem ipsum dolor sit amet, conse ctetuer adipi scing elit, sed diam nonummy nibh euismod tincidunt ut laoreet dolore magna. Ut wisi enim ad min im veniam, quis nostrud exerci tation ullamcorper. Susc ipit lobortis nisl ut aliq uip ex ea commodo consequat.

Lorem ipsum dolor sit amet, scing elit sed diam nonummy nibh. Euismod tincidunt ut laoreet dolore magna aliquam erat.

Dolor sit amet, consec tetuer adip iscing elit, sed diam nonummy nibh. Ut wisi enim ad min im veniam, quis nostrud exerci tation ullam. Corper suscipit lobortis nisl ut aliq uip ex ea commodo consequat; ipsum dolor sit amet, consectetuer adipiscing elit. Sed diam nonummy nibh euismod tincidunt ut laoreet dolore magna aliquam erat.

Ut wisi enim ad minim veniam, quis nostrud exerci tation ullamcorper suscipit. Lobortis nisl ut aliquip ex ea commodo consequat. Duis autem vel eum iriure dolor in hendrerit in tulp utate selit esse molestie consequat. Rel illum dolore eu feugiat nulla facilisis at vero eros et accumsan et iusto odio dig.

###

On the previous page is an example of a press release format and some things to remember.

- ○ Must be double spaced
- ○ Must be typed on a typewriter or computer
- ○ On top, put Contact: Your Name
- ○ In caps and on top, write FOR IMMEDIATE RELEASE
- ○ Put a catchy title on the press release
- ○ Must be on 8½ x 11 inch paper, white
- ○ A cover letter is recommended
- ○ Not longer than two pages
- ○ Always try to include a related photograph (Don't send a press release about a new tool and send in your photo, unless you are holding the tool).
- ○ Follow up: call the person you sent the release to one or two days after you send it in. Ask if they know when it might appear or why it might not. By calling you may be able to clear up the significance of this release, if they don't see it. By the way, they do expect you to call. If they say the release is going to be in on a certain day and it's not, call again. Remember, this is just one of many stories they are working on. Things do fall through the cracks.

ARTICLES

The difference between an article and a press release is that a press release is initially written by you, and the article is written by a

DEVELOPING YOUR NETWORKING SKILLS

writer for the publication. Often, if your press release is a newsworthy event, the paper will assign a writer to write an article out of it. Articles are very powerful tools. They are third party testimonials about you or your event. If someone from the news industry thinks it is important enough to write an article about, so will the readers. When they write an article, always ask if they will be using a photographer or if they would like you to supply some applicable photos or graphic material. By asking in this way, you are also suggesting that they do use photos, and this may go a long way toward getting them to do so.

SPONSORSHIP

This means that you or your company sponsors some type of event. This can be anything from a little league team or an after school raffle, to a scholarship or a major sports event. The more the event has to do with helping the community in some way, the better exposure it is for you and your company. If you don't know of an event to sponsor, talk to your local chamber of commerce, call a charity that you admire, or put together your own event. This can lead to a whole array of press that is worth its weight in dollars.

3   **Promotions**—whenever you have some type of sale or promotion going on, make sure you get your money's worth out of it. Exploit it for all it's worth and then some: Two for One, 10% Off, Free, Win this or that, Help Support..., Anniversary, and every holiday imaginable are all ways for you to promote your business. Did you know that the big department stores have some type of sale or promotion at least every six weeks. In fact, there

are actually more days out if the year that items are on sale than they are at regular price. Do these multi-million-dollar corporations know the power of promotions? You better believe it! Every business can have some type of promotion; you just have to be creative. Think, and then think some more.

Chapter 11

INTROVERT-EXTROVERT— DOES IT MATTER?

Over the years we have heard many excuses from others about why they won't network. Perhaps the most frequently cited reason is that the respondent considers himself too introverted to go out and meet people. At least one of the authors admitted in the Introduction to this book that he, too, is an introvert; and yet he is considered a highly successful networker. An outgoing personality and being comfortable as the "life of the party" may make it easier to meet people, but as we have said before, simply meeting people is not the same as networking. To a great extent, the ability to predict and motivate human behavior comes from the ability to recognize people as they are and deal with them as they are. An ability to size up the temperament of others provides you with clues as to how that person will behave and react toward other people.

In general, there are two major temperament classes—Introverts and Extroverts. Introverts express their emotions inwardly. They are concerned with the causes of action and generally tend to prefer detailed work. They do not care to work with or be with other people as much as they like to see the results of their own efforts. Introverts tend to gravitate toward occupations such as scientists, accountants and engineers.

Extroverts, on the other hand, express their emotions outwardly and are more concerned with action than with the causes behind the action. They are often inclined to put their ideas into motion without giving much consideration to the possible effects of that action. Extroverts make good actors, salespeople and politicians.

HOW INTROVERTS ACT

- ○ They are more comfortable writing than speaking.
- ○ They are often outspoken and can be direct and blunt in their comments.
- ○ They are easily embarrassed in front of a crowd.
- ○ They are often bashful, particularly in the presence of the opposite sex.
- ○ They tend to blush easily and do not laugh readily.

- They are thorough, meticulous and detail-oriented. They take good care of their possessions and can often be found straightening, adjusting and rearranging their desks or furniture.

- They are quite deliberate and take their time in speaking, dressing and in making decisions.

- They see arguments as intellectual exercises and enjoy participating in them.

- They tend to be perfectionists and spend a lot of time writing, rewriting and editing their written communications.

- They do not make new friends readily. They tend to have a wall of privacy which very few people are allowed to enter.

HOW INTROVERTS FEEL AND THINK

- They enjoy details and deliberate before making any decisions.
- By and large, they are worriers.
- They hold strong opinions, particularly about religion and politics.
- They do not like to take orders and want to know "why."
- They are inclined to be sensitive, and their feelings are easily hurt.
- They like to work alone and will persevere without asking for help.
- They often seem suspicious because they analyze and evaluate the motives of other people.

- They react strongly to praise and are highly motivated by sincere appreciation.

- They tend to avoid taking risks and prefer security.

- They like work that involves details and precision.

- They tend to choose intellectual pursuits over athletics and spectator sports.

- They spend a considerable amount of time daydreaming.

- They have a highly developed conscience and sense of responsibility.

HOW EXTROVERTS ACT

- They express themselves more by talking than in writing.

- They want to avoid hurting other people's feelings and are not strongly outspoken.

- They tend to be natural public speakers.

- They rarely blush and laugh readily.

- They often leave "loose ends" because they are not overly precise or meticulous.

- They move and speak quickly.

- They consider arguments to be confrontations and try to avoid them.

- They are not strongly concerned with details and tend not to rewrite their letters.
- They make friends easily and enjoy meeting people.

HOW EXTROVERTS FEEL AND THINK

- They are not concerned about details such as what to wear, where to meet, etc.
- They are not generally worriers.
- They are quite conservative about politics and religion.
- They accept orders or direction at face value and are more concerned with action than the reasons behind the action.
- They are usually not bothered by what is said about them and have the ability to let things roll off their back.
- They would rather work with other people than alone and ask for help fairly readily.
- They tend to accept others at face value rather than analyzing or evaluating their motives.
- They are generally not motivated by praise, but nonetheless seem to get their fair share.
- They are entrepreneurial in nature and willing to take risks.
- They tend to see things in the context of the "big picture" and can often overlook some details.

○ They prefer to be active in their leisure time rather than pursue intellectual activities.

○ They are not overly conscientious and can tend to rationalize.

A SELF EVALUATION

As you can see, in a psychological context, being an Introvert or an Extrovert has more to do with your temperament and how you process information than with being a wallflower or the life of the party. It is helpful, however, to have an understanding of your own preferences, an understanding which can help you be more successful in your approach to networking. A brief questionnaire follows that will help you ascertain some of your temperament qualities. In this survey, there is no such thing as a good or bad score. A score of 80 is no better than a score of 30. It simply means that you have a different way of taking in and processing data.

Instructions: Circle "Yes" or "No" to indicate how you would generally prefer to answer each question.

1 Would you rather stay at home and read than go out with a group of people?

Yes No

2 Do you like to do everything thoroughly and carefully, even when a less perfect job would be acceptable?

Yes No

INTROVERT-EXTROVERT—DOES IT MATTER?

3 Do you engage in comparison shopping before buying something fairly expensive?

Yes No

4 Do you like to do arithmetic or math problems?

Yes No

5 Have you lost out on something you wanted to do or buy because you did not make up your mind quickly enough?

Yes No

6 Do people consider you to be detail-oriented?

Yes No

7 Would you like to have things more settled and safe in your life with nothing to worry about as you look into the future?

Yes No

8 Do you like to tinker with or repair cars, appliances or other items around the house?

Yes No

9 Do you find yourself frequently dwelling on things you would like to see, to do or to have?

Yes No

10 Are you up in the clouds one day and down in the dumps the next?

Yes No

11 Do you blush easily?

Yes No

12 Are you hesitant about lending money, even to your friends?

Yes No

13 Do you allow people to cut in front of you in lines?

Yes No

14 Have you ever been afraid of losing a job because your work went badly?

Yes No

15 Are you annoyed when people watch you while you work?

Yes No

16 Can you continue doing routine work over long periods of time?

Yes No

17 Do you tend to keep quiet when you're out with people you don't know well?

Yes No

18 Does it bother you to have people talk about you?

Yes No

19 Do you like to read non-fiction books or attend lectures?

Yes No

20 Do you have strong religious or political convictions?

Yes No

21 Do you have a strong desire to feel more sure of yourself and to be more self-confident?

Yes No

INTROVERT-EXTROVERT—DOES IT MATTER?

22 Do you tend to "second guess" your decisions after you have made them?

Yes No

23 Do you like to tie up the loose ends and tend to the details of your work?

Yes No

24 Do you come right to the point and say what you have to say regardless of the consequences?

Yes No

25 Do you find other people so opinionated that it is often hard to reason with them?

Yes No

26 Are you usually more comfortable being a member rather than a leader of the organizations to which you belong?

Yes No

27 Does your personality stay pretty much the same, even in the face of dramatic experiences?

Yes No

28 Can you express yourself more easily by talking than in writing?

Yes No

29 Do you remember people well?

Yes No

30 Are you inclined to exaggerate about what you can do or about your experiences?

Yes No

31 Are you usually late for appointments?

Yes No

32 Is it easy for you to change your opinions or beliefs?

Yes No

33 Do you like to be busy with several things at the same time?

Yes No

34 Is it easy for you to get started on new projects?

Yes No

35 Are most people willing to cooperate with you and go along with your plans?

Yes No

36 Do you accept other people's mistakes good-naturedly?

Yes No

37 When you are out with your friends, are you usually the one who decides where to go and what to do?

Yes No

38 Do you like to have power or influence over people to get them to do what you want?

Yes No

INTROVERT-EXTROVERT—DOES IT MATTER?

39 Are you quick to say what you feel like saying?

Yes No

40 Are you inclined to take action without thinking much about the outcome?

Yes No

41 After you have completed the big and difficult parts of a job, do you dislike finishing up the odds and ends?

Yes No

42 Do you laugh easily?

Yes No

43 Do you care a lot about what other people think of you?

Yes No

44 Do you like to gamble or take risks?

Yes No

45 Are you comfortable entering a room where there are a lot of strangers?

Yes No

46 Do people say that you always want to have your own way?

Yes No

47 Do you prefer jobs where you work with other people?

Yes No

48 Are you usually the first one to speak when you meet people?

Yes No

49 Are you answering these questions quickly without much thought or deliberation?

Yes No

Scoring Key: Give yourself 2 points for each "Yes" answer on Questions 1–27; give yourself 2 points for each "No" answer on Questions 28–49. Add up all your points. If your score is between 49 and 0, you tend to be an Extrovert (the closer to 0 you are, the more Extroverted you are); if your score is between 50 and 100, you are an Introvert (the closer to 100 you are, the more Introverted you are). Again, remember, there are no better or worse scores. It is simply the way you tend to pick up and process information.

A good rule of thumb to follow when dealing with other people is to approach them as if they are Introverts. If you do so, the true Introverts will be comfortable, and the true Extroverts will soon clear up your misconceptions. To be a successful networker means that it is your responsibility to understand the other person; the other person should not necessarily understand you or your problems. To this end, we would suggest restating the Golden Rule: "Do unto others as they would want to have done unto them" (not as you would have done unto you or unto them). Apply patience and tolerance to your dealings with others. Set standards for them that apply to their capabilities, not yours. Recognize and take steps to overcome your own shortcomings rather than pointing out the mistakes of others. Learn to sustain yourself on less praise than you know you truly deserve. Remember, the farther up the ladder you climb, the fewer people there are to tell you what a good job you're doing. Save your praise for others. The true measure of your leadership as both a businessperson and a networker is your capacity to be sensitive to and understanding of the basic needs of others. People will be motivated to help you when they can be shown how to break through a barrier or to overcome a need in order to achieve a goal. Truly successful networkers have learned to capitalize on the synergy created by mutual goal achievement. Understanding how people are motivated will help you tap into their potential.

OUT OF YOUR COMFORT ZONE

Do you feel uncomfortable going up to people you don't know and introducing yourself? Is this why you don't go to mixers? Guess what? That is how 90 percent of the population feels. No one wants to feel they are forcing themselves on someone else. It is the fear of rejection that keeps us at bay. Have you seen the person at the mixers who can walk up to anyone and start a conversation and be liked instantly? You probably say to yourself, "I would love to have that ability but it is just not my personality to walk up to people I don't know and start a conversation. What would I say? What do you talk about?"

Nobody says you have to be as extroverted as the guy who is walking up to everyone and acting like he is the President of the event. However, you are there for a reason. When you go to a business networking event, you are there to network. You are there to mix with and meet people you don't know so you can establish new relationships and eventually get more business.

SUCCESSFUL BUSINESS NETWORKING

The way to do this is to take a small step out of your comfort zone and make a goal of meeting one new person at the next mixer you go to. Just one. Remember that everyone at that mixer is there for the same reason you are and has the same hesitations you do. If you approach someone new, you have done them a favor. If they are not taking the initiative, they will be thankful that you have because you have just made it easy for them to meet someone. You will be respected for your initiative. Your approach and conversation could go something like this:

YOU: "Excuse me. Hi, I'm Joe Smith."

PERSON: "Hello, I'm Linda Johnson."

YOU: "Hi Linda, it's nice to meet you."

PERSON: "It's nice to meet you, too."

YOU: "What is it that you do Linda?"

PERSON: "I own a print shop just down the road from here."

YOU: "Which one is that?"

PERSON: "A-1 Print & Copy on Main Street."

YOU: "The one across from the Bargain Furniture Store?"

PERSON: "Yeah, that's me."

YOU: "What type of printing do you do?"

PERSON: "We can do just about anything. In house we can do color brochures, booklets and the like. We can do full catalogs as well. We just send them out to our home office."

INTROVERT-EXTROVERT—DOES IT MATTER?

YOU: "You also do full business stationery supplies like letterhead, business cards, order forms and such?"

PERSON: "Oh sure, we do all that."

YOU: "In my business I run into people all the time who need all types of printing done. Maybe we could get together for lunch in the next week or two so I could find out a little more about what you do and see if I could refer some business your way."

PERSON: "Sounds great to me."

YOU: "Do you have a couple of business cards on you? Give me a few. I will be meeting with some of my clients early next week and I'd like to be able to give them your card."

PERSON: "Sure. Here, take five or six. By the way Joe, what do you do?"

YOU: "I'm a small business consultant. I work with companies to help them increase their bottom line by cutting costs and I help them market themselves better so they can dominate their market. Tell me, how do you find these business mixers?"

PERSON: "Usually they're fun, but I don't get much business out of them. That is, at least not until tonight."

Let's take a look at what has happened here. The person you approached is very appreciative that you introduced yourself. Not only has she met someone new, but you told her that you would be interested in sending her some business. Do you think this person is interested in speaking with you further? You better believe it. During this conversation, you concentrated on getting to know this person better and finding out about their business so you can help them. This person is now very motivated to sit down with you one-on-one.

If you were to end the conversation here or continue does not matter. You could end the conversation by giving her your business card and saying that you look forward to speaking with her in the next couple of days, or you could find out more about that person. What are her interests, hobbies, likes and dislikes. Does she play sports? Is she married, single, divorced, etc.? If you continue the conversation, the idea is to talk about them. Ask them interesting and significant questions about themselves. This puts them at ease and creates a comfortable atmosphere. It shows that you are a giving person, a good listener who is not just a salesperson looking to see what you can get from them. When you find a common interest, you need to let them know that, no matter what it is. The idea is to see how you can help anyone you speak with. Take a sincere interest in getting to know them better and seeing what you can do for them.

Chapter 12

LISTEN TO OTHERS IF YOU WANT TO BE HEARD

The more people know about you, the better able they will be to provide you with good referrals. Likewise, the more you know about the other people in your network, the more you will be able to refer them, which will make them want to refer even more business your way. The key to knowing about each other is to really listen to each other.

Listening and hearing are not the same thing. More than 26 million Americans suffer from hearing loss. Poor hearing can often be improved by wearing a hearing aid. Unfortunately, there is no similar mechanical device to improve listening skills. Failure to listen is often the result of a closed mind: "Sure, I hear you talking, but my mind is already made up." Or it may be caused by a lack of respect for the speaker: "I know you're talking, but your opinion doesn't really matter." And in many cases, just as with hearing loss, listening problems become worse as we get older, and, as we become more set in our ways, the less we are able to accept different points of view.

Ironically, one of the biggest challenges to our listening skills is the fact that we live in what is called "the information age." It is an age dominated by computers, electronic data and telecommuting. As a result, we have isolated ourselves and tend to associate only with people who are just like us. Rarely do we make opportunities to verbally interact with or listen to people who differ from us professionally, socially, culturally, ethnically or sexually. In a time of sound bites and spin doctors, we place high value on glib and dynamic speakers. Good listeners, on the other hand, because they are often quiet, are labeled as unfriendly or uninteresting.

10 TECHNIQUES OF A GOOD LISTENER

Successful networkers realize that good listening skills are the basis of good communication, and they are willing to invest the time and effort it takes to be good listeners. Here are the top ten techniques:

1 What's in it for me?

2 Pay attention to what is said, not how it is said.

3 Talk less, listen more.

4 Expect the unexpected.

LISTEN TO OTHERS IF YOU WANT TO BE HEARD

5 Keep the speaker interested.

6 Don't get distracted.

7 Be aware of your blind spots.

8 Ask for clarification.

9 Take notes if material is complex.

10 Rephrase what the speaker has said.

1. What's in it for me?—it is a plain and simple fact that you will listen more attentively if you believe that you are going to derive value out of what is being said. When another person is talking, pay attention for worthwhile ideas that you may be able to use for yourself. Of course you want to know about the other person and what they do so you can refer them to a third party, but the best way to remember what the speaker does is by identifying ways to relate what they do to what you do or to things you already know something about. Finding areas of common interest between yourself and the speaker will heighten your awareness of what they are saying and increase your memory of their message.

2. Pay attention to what is said, not how it is said—some people have voices that seem to grate on your ears like squeaky chalk on a blackboard. Some speak so slowly that they (and you) seem to fall asleep between the words, while others rattle off sentences like staccato bursts from a machine gun. Learn not to let the speaker's speech, voice, personality, annoying habits, etc., prevent you from listening to the actual message. Most people are not skilled speakers and are not very good at getting their ideas across. To be a good listener, focus on the content of what is said rather than on the style or delivery with which it is said.

3. Talk less, listen more—active listening means letting the speaker finish speaking before putting your mouth in gear. Be careful not to jump to conclusions before the speaker has concluded. Don't think about what you are going to say, how you are going to refute the speaker or how to recall contrary data. Rather, devote your attention to the ideas being presented. You'll have your chance to talk, and you will be better prepared to do so if you have all the information. Also, remember that most people will lose their train of thought if they are interrupted. So by trying to help the speaker complete their message, you may actually derail it. Let the speaker finish unless they ask a question or request a response.

4. Expect the unexpected—in ordinary situations, most speakers are generally not well organized, nor do they follow an outline to ensure a logical progression of their remarks. Therefore, you have to avoid the tendency to mentally or physically take notes in such a way that you provide a structure or meaning the speaker never intended. Anticipating what the speaker is going to say can result in your hearing what you expect to hear rather than what is actually being said.

5. Keep the speaker interested—active listening requires work and involves your entire body. You can let the speaker know that you are interested in what is being said by maintaining eye contact with the speaker. Smiles, nods and facial expressions all demonstrate that you are paying attention and that you are at least willing to hear what the speaker has to say, without necessarily indicating that you accept or agree with the speaker's point of view.

6. Don't get distracted—ringing telephones, beeping computers, interruptions of all sorts—the world is full of distractions which make it difficult to listen well. Good listeners have learned the

LISTEN TO OTHERS IF YOU WANT TO BE HEARD

importance of removing obstacles by closing the door, disconnecting the phone, requesting privacy, etc. If you can't remove the distractions, learn to ignore them so you can focus your attention on the speaker's central ideas.

7. Be aware of your blind spots—each and every person has certain likes and dislikes, things they are comfortable discussing and issues they would rather avoid. Good listeners are aware of their prejudices and take care not to "tune out" when a speaker touches a sensitive area. Be careful that you don't close your mind to different interests, goals, values or experiences with which you may not agree. Permit yourself to be open to new ideas. Who knows, you might just learn something.

8. Ask for clarification—if you're not sure of or are confused about something the speaker said, ask them to clarify it. Do so respectfully without inferring that the lack of clarity is the speaker's fault. Statements like, "I (or you) don't know what you're talking about," or, "You're confusing me," are not conducive to good communications or relationships.

9. Take notes if the material is complex—you will remember much more of what is said if you take notes during the speaker's presentation, especially if the material is complex or filled with details. If you think the speaker will be disturbed by or find your note-taking inappropriate, ask their permission before taking out your pen and notebook. Make sure you frame your request in a positive way, such as, "This is really important, and I don't want to forget it, so is it okay if I write it down?" rather than saying something like, "I don't want you saying that I screwed up what you said, so I better write it down."

10. Rephrase what the speaker said—to make sure you've understood the speaker correctly, rephrase what you heard the other person say and ask them if you got the message right. When rephrasing, don't add editorial comments or try to psychoanalyze the speaker. However, do let the speaker know that you listened to both the content and the intent of the message. Once you understand both, then you can say that you really listened.

Most people listen at about 25 percent efficiency. You can also think about four times faster than you speak, so it is easy to be inattentive. With training and practice, however, you can raise your comprehension and retention levels considerably. It will take work to improve your skills in this area, but you can't be a good networker if you're not a good listener. Remember and practice the old adage, "You've got two ears and one mouth; use them proportionately."

Chapter 13

LEARNING TO TALK GOOD

If you would rather face root canal work without Novocaine than make a speech, you are not alone. Did you know that the number one fear in the world is public speaking? Number two is death by fire or drowning! For most people, the very thought of having to speak in front of a group brings on a sense of panic and gastric distress. But just as with death and taxes, chances are that you will not be able to avoid having to speak in public at some point during your career.

Good speaking skills are practically a must to be a good networker. Let's face it, you can't network without talking to people, and the ability to address a group and to do so capably is one of, if not the best, means of attracting new members into your network.

SUCCESSFUL BUSINESS NETWORKING

Peter Drucker, the well-known management guru, has said, "You cannot build personal performance by focusing on weaknesses. You can improve personal performance only by focusing on strengths." So to begin with, if you want to improve your public speaking abilities, start by assessing your strengths rather than concentrating on your weaknesses. How do you do that? Well, let's look at some of the techniques used by professional speakers.

HOW TO BE P.R.E.P.A.R.E.D.

We'll let you in on a secret. Although the authors of this book are both members of the National Speakers Association and have qualified to be Professional Speakers, there is never a time immediately prior to stepping up to the microphone that we are not nervous. It is only natural to feel a certain amount of anxiety—after all, your heart beats faster when you engage in public speaking than at any other time in your life. The secret is not to be consumed by your fear. Instead of thinking of that fluttering feeling in your stomach as butterflies, think of it as "flutter-bys." Accept the fact that it's okay to be afraid, and then let go of it rather than hanging on to the fear. Perhaps the best way to do this is to be P.R.E.P.A.R.E.D.

P = Plan

Proper planning can eliminate the fear of going into a presentation unprepared. The planning process includes such things as:

○ Why are you making the presentation?—that is, what do you want to make the audience think, feel or do as a result of having listened to you?

LEARNING TO TALK GOOD

205

○ Who are your speaking to?—that is, what are the demographics of the audience. What do they have in common? What are their interests likely to be? Why are they gathered in this particular place at this particular time?

○ What are you going to say?—it's always a good idea to have something to say before you start speaking. Unfortunately, far too many people seem to engage their mouths before putting their brain in gear. You don't want to be thought of in this light. Put together an outline of what you want to say that will include the following components:

Introduction—this can be used by another person who is going to introduce you in a formal presentation setting or can help you set the stage for helping your audience to understand why they should want to listen to what you have to say.

Grabber—this is another word for having a powerful beginning to your presentation. You want to generate a sense of emotion and feeling on the part of your audience. You don't want to be a boring drone or start off by putting your audience to sleep.

Bridge—this means drawing a natural progression from your opening grabber to the body of your speech. During the bridge, you want to let the audience know that you relate to them and their needs.

Make your point—now that the audience knows why they should listen to you (your introduction), you've got their attention (the grabber), and they know that you can relate to their needs (the bridge), you can now come to the main body of your speech, and they will be ready to hear it.

Back up your claims—if you make any claims or promises during the course of your presentation, make sure you are able to back them up. This could be by means of reports, statistics, third-party testimonials, etc.

Close—your ending should reinforce your message and leave your audience with the desire to think, feel or do what you had in mind when you began the planning process by asking yourself, "Why are you making the presentation?"

R = Rehearse

To be a good speaker or to be good at anything in life requires practice, practice and more practice. Professional speakers, like professional athletes, practice until they get it right, and then they continue to practice some more. Some of the practice techniques used by professional speakers include:

○ **Internalize, don't memorize**. Write out, then read and reread your entire speech until it becomes second nature to you. You can still have your notes or even the full text in front of you, but your presentation should come across naturally and conversationally. If you plan on reading your speech verbatim to the audience, you run the risk of speaking in a monotone voice and putting them to sleep. If you try to memorize your speech, you run the risk of forgetting parts of it or tripping over your words.

○ **Get someone to critique you**. If you've been called upon to make a speech, and especially if some of your present or prospective customers or networkers are going to be there, you can't afford to take the risk of making a presentation that doesn't make sense. Practice giving your speech in front of two or three members of your current network, preferably those who share some of the characteristics of the audience you will be addressing. Ask them to critique your speech, both from the standpoint of content and delivery.

○ **Use a video camera**. Most of us have absolutely no idea how we look or come across to other people. We probably have several annoying little habits that we are not even conscious of, but which can be very disconcerting to an audience. By videotaping both your rehearsals and your actual presentations, you'll be in a position to identify areas where you might need some improvement, as well as strengths on which you can capitalize.

○ **Tape record your presentations**. Even if you don't have access to a video recorder, almost anyone can get their hands on a tape recorder. Just as most of us don't know what we look like to other people, very few of us know how we sound. Bear in mind that most tape recorders will not give you an exact representation of your voice, so don't be surprised at what you sound like. What the tape recorder can be used for is to identify how you are using your voice and what you are saying, not the tone of your voice. Listen for pitch and emphasis and a variety of tones as opposed to a monotone recitation. See if tape recording your speech makes you want to listen to it. If not, at least it can give you an idea of what to work on.

○ **Practice eye focus**. You may remember your public speaking teacher in high school advising you to focus your eyes slightly above the heads of the people in the back row of the audience. Theoretically this was supposed to help you to stay calm, since you wouldn't have to look at anyone. We disagree totally with this concept. As professional speakers, the authors do not speak to groups of people. We speak to individuals who happen to be gathered in a room at the same time. Instead of focusing on no one, practice focusing on one person at a time and move your eyes from one person to another, back and forth from right to left, from front to rear. By doing so, everyone in attendance will get the impression that you are speaking directly to them. There is no better way to develop a rapport with your audience than by making eye contact with them as individuals.

E = Edit

As a speaker, you have 20 percent of your audience's attention 40 percent of the time. That's because people need time to process what they hear, so your speech needs to be interesting, and you need to be animated and to repeat the important parts of your speech.

Avoid the pride of authorship pitfall, that is, don't assume that just because you thought of it and wrote it down, that it belongs in your speech. During the rehearsal and critiquing phases, you are bound to identify rough spots in your speech. Don't hesitate to add, subtract and revise your speech until you've got it right. Here are some tips that can help you with this process:

○ **Focus on the audience**. The purpose of your speech is not to hear yourself talk, but to meet the needs of your audience. Edit your speech so that you provide your audience with what they need to know. Doing so will make them want to listen to you.

LEARNING TO TALK GOOD

209

○ **KISS your speech**. One of the capital rules in speech making is to Keep It Short and Simple (KISS). Your speech should be short enough to engage the audience's attention throughout its duration and simple enough that the average member of the audience can understand it. To properly KISS your speech goes back to having a thorough understanding of who is in your audience, why they are there and what you want to say to them. During your editing process, look for the use of slang, acronyms or technical jargon that may not be familiar to your listeners.

○ **Provide the audience with a map**. This means editing your speech so that your audience knows where you are taking them and where they are at various points along the way. Jumping from point to point or place to place is a good way to lose an audience in a hurry.

○ **Have proof for your claims**. The editing process is a good place to make sure that you have proof or back up for any claims or assertions you have made during your presentation. If you are quoting statistics, for example, make sure you know where the numbers have come from. You may not have to mention the source during your presentation, but be prepared to respond to any challenges that may come from the audience during a question and answer period.

○ **Use variety and movement**. Various market researchers and psychologists have told us that the average attention span of an adult American is seven minutes; therefore, unless you want your audience turning you off or tuning you out, you need to add variety and movement to your speech. Use gestures that are normal and natural, and use various vocal inflections during the course of your speech.

P = Psyche Yourself Up

Get yourself psyched up and ready to speak before you begin speaking. You have between eight and 15 seconds to make a first impression on your audience. You cannot afford to waste that time. Acknowledge your fear and work through it. As we said before, even professional speakers have a certain amount of fear which they must overcome before beginning a presentation. Some techniques we have found helpful include:

- Stand up straight and give the physical appearance of being confident. Your posture can trick your central nervous system into feeling a level of comfort you may not really have.

- Force yourself to breathe slowly and deeply.

- Smile. It helps control the release of the enzyme that causes fear.

- Yawn to open the throat and increase your supply of oxygen (of course, you want to yawn discreetly—after all, you don't want the audience to think that you're bored by your speech before you even begin).

- Let the butterflies be flutter-bys. Keep your inner voice quiet during your presentation.

- Visualize yourself as an effective and successful speaker. Imagine the accolades and applause you are going to receive before you begin speaking. In speaking as in all of life, if you view yourself as a success or as a failure, you're right.

- You are the expert. Remember, you have been invited or have volunteered to speak, which means that you know something

LEARNING TO TALK GOOD

that the audience wants to learn. You are there to convey knowledge to them or to motivate the audience, not the other way around. Keep this in mind, and it will go a long way toward helping you be more effective.

○ You don't have to be brilliant. You don't have to be quotable to be memorable. Research conducted by Toastmaster International has demonstrated that there are actually three major components of a speech that must be used if your speech is to have impact and to be understood, believed and remembered. The importance of these three components varies with the length of the presentation as follows:

	20-Minute Presentation	2-Minute Presentation
Words used	15%	7%
Voice	45%	38%
Body	40%	55%

As you can see, the tone of your voice and your body language are more important to the success of your speech than the words you use. In the words of the poet Ralph Waldo Emerson, "What you are speaks so loudly that I cannot hear what you are saying."

Again drawing on research performed by Toastmaster International and the National Speakers Association, there are five key qualities that a business audience looks for in a speaker.

1 Enthusiastic—comes from the Greek word *entheos*, meaning the god within, that is, the belief that the speaker has in his or her own message and the conveyance of that belief to the audience.

2 Dynamic—the speaker must have a sense of purpose and be animated in delivery.

3 Focused on what the audience needs to know, not on the speaker's desire to talk.

4 Comfortable, that is, the speaker must appear to be at ease and in charge.

5 Real—you must be what you talk about, and you must be human. In other words, you've got to walk the talk.

A = Accept your uniqueness and accentuate your strengths

All of us have from time to time heard speeches or seen speakers who have moved us tremendously. We sit in the audience and think, "Wow, if only I could do that. I would like to be just like that person." Perhaps you've even decided to try to model your presentations after a particular speaker's style. But the fact is, you are not and never will be that other person. You are you, and that's plenty good enough.

Remember that it is you that the audience is there to hear and see. Unless you are an impressionist, they are not there to watch you try to be someone else. It is your knowledge of the subject matter that they want to have conveyed to them. It is your personal style and uniqueness which will make you real, and therefore, more acceptable to the audience.

Also don't forget to capitalize on the strengths that you possess. Your peculiar tone of voice and speech patterns can be just the thing to set you apart from anyone else. If you think of your differences in a positive way, they can become your strengths rather than eroding your self-confidence. There is an old story about the rabbi Souza whose disciples asked why he taught them in a manner different from other rabbis. He told his students, "When I die and stand before the Lord, He will not say to me, 'Souza, why were you not Moses, or why were you not David?' No, the Lord will say to me, 'Souza, why were you not fully Souza?'" In the same way, you must be fully you to be effective as a speaker.

R = Referrals are your goal

Unless you have been specifically invited to make a sales pitch, your presentation should be thought of as a means of providing you with an opportunity to address a group of people who might be in a position to refer business to you. Too often we have seen audiences completely tune out when the speaker uses the podium as a platform to try to sell his or her own goods and services, rather than presenting objective information during a presentation.

If you remember to think of your presentation in terms of trying to impress only one or two people in the audience sufficiently to make them want to become part of your network, you will find that you will be much more relaxed than if you think of the speech in terms of trying to sell yourself to everyone there. Also, because you are using your speech to add to your network, don't forget to use the time after your speech to talk one-on-one with members of the audience who might approach you. Be ready to distribute your business cards (not sales brochures—save those for another time) and to collect the business cards of those whom you met. Remember, too, to follow up with a note or a phone call within a few days of your speech to all of those people whose cards you have collected. You can also ask the organization sponsoring your speech to provide you with a list of names and addresses of the attendees. A brief note to each of them, along with your business card, will not only help to reinforce your message, but will also keep your name in front of them.

E = Evaluations can be helpful

Prior to your speech, ask the sponsoring organization if they will be distributing evaluation forms to the audience. If so, ask the sponsor if you can receive a copy of each of the evaluations. If the sponsoring organization does not plan to utilize evaluation forms, ask if you can distribute your own. The goal of having your presentation evaluated is to help you identify those areas where the audience thought you were strong and right on target, as well as those parts of your speech where you might need some improvement. If the evaluators provide their name and address on the form, it is even more helpful, since you then have an opportunity to correspond with them, thereby letting them know that you are interested in what they have to say.

When reviewing evaluations of your speech, it helps to bear in mind that no matter who you are or what you have to say, approximately 20 percent of the audience is simply not going to like you. Of the remaining 80 percent, only half will have listened closely enough to provide an objective evaluation. It is among the few who are open to your message and who have paid sufficient attention that you will find the kind of people you would want to have in your network. By incorporating their comments into your future presentations and by letting them know that you plan to do so, you will have taken the first step toward making them feel that they really do want to be part of your network.

If formal evaluations are not possible for you to conduct, you can at least talk to members of the audience after your speech. By watching the audience's reaction during your presentation, you will have identified those who seem to have been paying particular attention to you and with whom you seem to have struck a chord. Search out these people after your speech, and ask them to provide you with informal feedback. Most, if not all of them, will be more than happy to help you. Even if their comments seem negative at face value, you should not let that get you down. After all, you can turn the situation into a positive experience by letting the person know that you appreciate their thoughts and that hopefully, in the future, you will be able to do a better job with your presentations as a result of their suggestions. By letting the other person know that you respect their opinion rather than becoming argumentative or defensive, you are much more likely to win that person over to your side and may even turn them into one of your fans.

D = Dress for success

One of the best pieces of advice we have received during our speaking careers is to "Dress one notch above your audience." You don't want to be so out of touch with the dress code of your audience that you stand out like a sore thumb, but you do want the audience to recognize that you are the speaker and, therefore, the expert. Dressing too casually can detract from the perception you are trying to convey as an authority and can make it much less likely that the audience will perceive you as a leader. This is why, prior to the date of your presentation, it is important to be in contact with the sponsoring organization to find out what the dress code will be for the event at which you will be speaking. More than once we have seen an otherwise outstanding speaker lose their audience by showing up in a business suit at a black tie event. Even at programs where the audience will be dressed in casual attire, a sport coat or blazer is always appropriate for the speaker. Clothes may not make the speaker, but clothes can break the speaker.

Be prepared by being P.R.E.P.A.R.E.D. even when speaking informally. Although you may be called upon very infrequently to make a formal presentation or speech, the information provided in this chapter is useful in all types of oral communications, whether in front of a large audience, at a mixer, or when simply introducing yourself to a few people at a party. Networking requires communication, and most communication is in the form of conversation. Practice the tips and techniques presented above, and pretty soon you, like Larry King, can talk to anybody about anything at any time.

Part VI

NETWORK SALES & MARKETING

SECRET 5:

HELP YOURSELF BY HELPING OTHERS

Chapter 14

WORK YOUR NETWORKS SINCERELY

MOVE 'EM UP

So far you have organized everyone you know into one of your 5 networking categories, evaluated what they have been giving you, researched who you need in your Primary Network and reviewed and/or learned the skills necessary to network. Now it is time to put your skills into action and move the associates you have in your lower level networks up to the higher ones. Until now we have done a lot of research and paperwork. Now it is time to network and put it all into action.

First we need to discuss Level Jumping. This is when you want to bring someone from your lower level networks to a higher one and "Jump" the level in between. For instance, you may have found that you need a good personal injury attorney in your Primary Network. However, the only one you know is currently in the Dormant Networker category. How do we get her up to the Primary level? First you must understand that it does not happen overnight. It is important to remember that just because you may place someone in one of your higher networking levels, it doesn't mean anything unless they feel that they are that close to you as well. Just because you call me and we go to lunch does not mean that I consider you a close associate. That kind of commitment takes time. To bring someone up a level or two takes consistent commitment from you to show that you are sincere in having them as an associate. You must demonstrate this commitment not only by keeping in contact with them or having them over for dinner, but by actually doing something for them. When I see that you are a sincerely giving person and that we have a genuine working relationship, then I will accept you as a close associate of mine.

It's similar to when you are dating someone and you decide that this person is the one for you. You go head over heals into the relationship and tell the person how much they mean to you and how you want to really get serious and that you think you are in love with them. But they are not quite ready for this type of commitment and don't share your feelings at this time. You then realize that you have to take it slow and build this relationship over time. You have to remain patient, let the person see that you are sincere, and let them fall for you as you have for them. I'm sure we have all had this experience. Well, building a relationship with a Networking Associate is the same. Make a commitment to the relationship, but remember that you must let your associate develop the belief in you that you have in them.

So how do we Jump Levels with an associate?

1 Contact them and tell them what you want to do

2 Meet and discuss the plan

3 Build a profile

4 "DO" something for your associate

5 Keep a record of your accomplishments

6 When they ask, say, "Nothing"

1. Contact them and tell them what you want to do—in an earlier chapter we gave an example of how to do this. Call your old associate and tell them what you are looking to do and why.

Do you feel awkward calling someone you haven't called in a while for the purpose of building up your network? Well, don't. Remember, you are calling them to reestablish a relationship. You want to see if you can set up a mutually beneficial networking relationship. When you get together with the person and when you first speak to them on the telephone, be honest.

FRANK: "Mary, how are you? This is Frank De Raffele calling. Long time no talk."

MARY: "Frank, oh my gosh. How are you? It's been so long."

FRANK: "Too long. How's things...your family, business?"

MARY: "Things are great. Steven got promoted and is doing lot of traveling. The kids are in middle school now. It's a lot harder, but they love it."

FRANK: "What are your kids' names again? How old are they now?"

MARY: "Joseph is 12 and in eighth grade, and Sylvia is 10 and in fifth grade."

FRANK: "Wow, does time fly."

MARY: "I know, I just can't believe it."

FRANK: "You know, I was looking through my address book and transferring names into my Networking System, and I came across your name. I felt so guilty for not calling you in so long that I wanted to give you call and see if we could get together for lunch."

MARY: "I'd love to. What is a Networking System?"

FRANK: "I've found a new way to organize my business where I organize all the people I know in my Networking System. This allows me to keep in contact with the people in my network that I consider very important to me in a much more timely fashion. I have what I consider my Primary Network. These are the people of primary importance to my personal and business life. You are one of the people I'd like to have in that network. I've always admired and respected your work ethic and professionalism, as well as your friendship. Having a Primary Network allows me to prioritize my life according to who I really want to help and spend my time with. I would like to get together, besides to just catch up, to see how I can help send you some business or at least keep my ear open for something of value to you."

MARY: "Sounds great to me. But only on one condition."

FRANK: "Name it."

MARY: "You have to show me this Networking System. It sounds like something I could definitely use."

FRANK: "That's a deal. So when can we get together?"

This is almost the exact conversation I had with one of my Networking Associates when I called them after not speaking with them for 18 months. It is a good example because just about all of the phone calls I have made go pretty much like this. The best is when the person wants to get on the same Networking System that I am on. This means I will be a part of their Primary Network, and I have already helped them in a big way to get their business more organized, effective and profitable.

2. First meet and discuss the plan—it is important to get together with your associate as soon as possible. By getting together you both have taken the first step to committing to the relationship. To give up time for someone else is no small thing. At this meeting you want to explain that you are looking to get to know them better because you would like to try to find them some business. This makes you look good—to your clients, other associates, friends and family—because it puts you in the position of being a person who wants to help. People will rely on your judgment and connections to help them, and they will in turn want to help you because they want access to your connections. You may want to set a regular schedule with your associates to touch base or get together.

3. Build a profile—you want to build a profile on each of your associates. This is what we call "Make Your Associates Your F.A.B.U.L.O.S. Networkers." F.A.B.U.L.O.S. is an acronym that represents all the different information you want to know about your associates. (Yes, I know it's spelled wrong.)

Family

Activities

Business

Uniqueness

Loves

Organizations

Sports

If you don't have a good program in your computer to store this information, you can use this F.A.B.U.L.O.S. Networker Sheet.

○ **Family**—first you want to know about their immediate family: spouse, children (each one), mother, father, mother-in-law, father-in-law, dogs, cats, birds and pet rock, if appropriate. In this section you want to have as much vital information about their family as possible: birthdays, anniversaries, deaths, reasons for deaths, ages, types of dogs, cats, etc. What is their relationship with their parents or kids? Do they speak? Do you know why not? Don't assume anything. If you happen to make a big deal about their parents and they don't get along with their parents, you haven't scored any points. If you know it is a sore subject, stay away from it. Where do their kids go to school? Do they go to school? Do they not have kids because they don't want to or because they couldn't? Again, probably another sore subject. Build this part of the profile as accurately as possible.

WORK YOUR NETWORKS SINCERELY

F.A.B.U.L.O.S. NETWORKER SHEET

Names:_____Street Address _____

City_____State_____Zip_____

Business Phone:_____Home Phone:_____

Birthday_____Nationality_____Place of Birth_____

Parents Status _____

Preferred Color_____Flower_____Place_____

Other _____

FAMILY

Spouse: _____Birthday_____Astrological Sign_____

Birthstone_____Nationality_____Place of Birth_____

Parents Status _____

Preferred Color_____Flower_____Place_____

Children: Name(s) _____

   Age(s)_____

   Status _____

ACTIVITIES _____

BUSINESS _____

Position_____Started working in this profession in _____

Past jobs _____

Future Goals _____

Other _____

UNIQUENESS _____

Your Opinion _____

Their Opinion _____

LOVES _____

ORGANIZATIONS _____

SPORTS _____

Refer to it often because you will forget. As your network grows your memory will fade. That's what good records are for. Any information you gather about their family is good for you to know. Does their spouse hate the color blue? If you know this, you know never to send a present that is blue. See what we mean?

○ **Activities**—is this person a little league coach, scout master, cheerleading coach? The activities people are involved in tell a lot about them. People will usually coach a sport they enjoy themselves. They may be involved in a local theater group, teach a painting class or work with the homeless. When you know the activities someone is involved in, you have a way you can score points with them through something they obviously enjoy. All of us are extremely busy. In order to take time out of your day to dedicate to an activity means you must have a good reason for doing so. If you coach a team, you probably want to spend more time with your child, enjoy the sport you're coaching and enjoy being with children. If I know that you coach a little league team, maybe instead of getting tickets for you and your wife to go to a play, I will get passes for you and your team to a major or minor league baseball game. Never underestimate the power of enhancing relationships through the activities someone is involved in. Instead of sending a generic holiday card or present, you could send something that has a real flavor of what they enjoy. During regular conversations, you can get away from talking about work and ask about their organization, team, or group and see how you can help. For you to take time for something they are taking time for goes a long way.

- **Business**—what is their exact position with the company? How long have they been there? How many years of experience do they have? What exactly does the company do? What type of clients do they work with? What is a good referral for them? Any and all information you find out about their business should go in this section. The better educated and informed you are about each of your Networking Associate's businesses, business practices, clients, specials, etc., the easier it will be for you to find ways to help them and hopefully increase their business. Some of this, initially, can be learned from their brochures, catalogues and press kits. Most of it will come with time. The more time you spend with each associate, the more information you will have about their business. What we've found is that the more business information we gain on each associate, the more we can be creative about how we can help these people create strategic alliances within our own network. It's extremely beneficial to all involved when you can serve as a catalyst for new business relationships for people within your own network. They both benefit, and you have the gratitude of the two parties. Keep adding information on your associates because you never know when you are going to be able to create that ultimate referral for them.

- **Uniqueness**—what do you think makes this associate unique? What does this associate think really makes them unique? This is a very revealing bit of information. You may view one of your associates in a particular way and find them unique in a very different way than they see themselves. Before you ask them about this, you should write down your own opinion. Then compare notes. When you ask your associate what they think makes them unique compared to the other people in business today, don't let them get away with, "My hard work," or "My honesty." This may be true, but see if you can get them to think about it. If you respond to their statement with, "Yes, I could see that. What else do you think really sets you apart?" or something as simple as, "Your honesty," make sure you phrase it as a statement, not a question. This cues them to continue speaking. What you are really aiming for here is for them to possibly come to some realization they haven't had before. You may be able to help them develop a new way to market themselves with their unique qualities. We are not talking about the unique qualities of their business, but their unique qualities as individuals.

○ **Loves**—what is their passion? Your associate may be an outstanding consultant, chiropractor, plumber or salesperson, but what is their real love? Have they wanted to dance at Radio City Music Hall? Do they love to hike and climb mountains? Is their desire to scale Mt. Everest? Very few of us are living our dreams. Is the quiet accountant or computer programmer in your network a ferocious warrior and high level black belt in some martial art? Knowing what someone loves tells a lot about that person. They may be living their business life in one way, but have a very different life goal. By knowing a person's true love, you can contribute to that in many little ways: articles you find in a newspaper or magazine; lectures being given by someone in that field; little knick-knack gifts that would bring a smile to their face in the middle of the work day. Contribute to a person's loves, and you have touched their soul. If you can empower someone's passion for what they do, it will have a greater

WORK YOUR NETWORKS SINCERELY

impact than any referral worth any dollar amount. You have touched them in their heart and where they really live.

○ **Organizations**—what professional organizations do they belong to? What volunteer organizations are they part of? People's involvement in different organizations gives them another network of associates. You may read in the paper one day of a person you have been trying to get in to see for some business being appointed to the board of a certain organization. By knowing your networker's involvement in organizations, you may be able to call on one of your associates to pull some strings for you and introduce you. You may also create an opportunity by putting together an organization with a particular profession, group or situation within your contact of networks.

Helping out an organization that one of your networkers is affiliated with gives you the opportunity to make your associate look great in front of their whole organization. Even if you arranged the whole thing yourself, give the accolades to your associate.

"A few weeks ago when I was speaking with Amanda, she was telling me about the great things this organization does and how important it was to her to make your children's drive very successful. I decided to speak with my friends here at the shop. I'm happy that we are able to present you with this donation, and would like to give the credit to Amanda for being the type of person she is."

Do you think this moves Amanda up a few notches in the eyes of her peers in this organization? Absolutely. Does she attribute that to you? Right again. Don't just do for your associates; do for the things your associates care about.

○ **Sports**—talk about passions! How possessive do people get about their sports? If you can contribute to making an associate more successful at their particular sport, you have pretty much scored a home run, excuse the pun. If they're a golfer, they're a fanatic; there are no two ways about it. In fact, the Latin derivation for golfer is *Golforus Fanaticus*. Pretty much anything you send them that can cut strokes, increase their distance or give them an excuse for not playing well, would be more than appreciated. Find out what your associate's favorite sports are now and which sports they played in the past. Were they the star field hockey player, quarterback of the football team, team captain, All American? Sports include everything from baseball, basketball and football to badminton, ping pong and billiards. For all you know, they may be making more money playing pool on the weekends or betting on their favorite sports than they are at their career. Find out what they enjoy, and keep your antennas up.

This profile is a very powerful tool. A Networking Associate's profile is a living, breathing thing. Every time you learn something new about this person, add it to their profile. This gives you more ways to positively affect your associates' lives. Clipping out articles and sending them to your associates lets them know you are thinking of them. For example, you find out that one of your associates has a true love for chess and has always wanted to meet Bobby Fisher. One day you read in the newspaper that Bobby Fisher is coming to town. You can let that person know, get them tickets to see him or go yourself and get an autographed photo. Whatever it is, you can help make a difference in your associates' lives in simple ways that they will more than appreciate. And you do all of this so that they know how sincere you are in helping them. This leads to dramatic relationship building.

WORK YOUR NETWORKS SINCERELY 231

4. "DO" something for your associates—put your networks in place and see how you can help each networker. Find out about your associates—information, contacts, connections and referrals. When you get referrals for them, try to provide a greater number of Complex Referrals than Compound and a greater number of Compound Referrals than Simple. Whatever it is you would like from your associates, make sure that is what you are giving. Because you have initiated this networking relationship, you must lead by example. It is up to you to show your associates exactly what you mean when you talk about having them in your upper level networks. They consider you the expert in this area. Show them that you are.

5. Keep a record of your accomplishments—in your profile for each associate, leave space for what you have done for them in areas other than business. For example, what type of help have you given them on a personal or family level, and how has it worked out? This inventory lets you know how you are doing. Down the road you can check back with them about the help you have given and ask how it worked out. This will serve as your own personal score card.

6. When they ask, say, "Nothing"—as your associates see the commitment you have to them, they will want to help you in any way they can. When they ask you, "Steve, what exactly is it I can do for you?" Unless you really need something they have, say, "Nothing." You are developing these relationships for long-term business success. The more deposits you make into that Networking Associate's "Trust Fund," the bigger withdrawal you will be able to make when needed down the road. You want all of your associates working to give you a Complex Referral. To have a group of people willing to pull out all the stops to help you is the ultimate result of unselfish networking. You may never use it. The idea is to have it there, just in case. A lot of times my response will be, "I really don't need anything right now. I appreciate your offer, though. If you come across anyone you think could use my services, please recommend me. Besides that, I really feel good knowing that I've been able to help you out." After all, that's what networking is all about. Right?

Chapter 15

TURN YOUR NETWORKERS AND CUSTOMERS INTO RAVING FANS

Don't be content to simply move the people in your networks up from category to category. Even those you consider to be Primary Networkers can become more enthusiastic about you and your services. Your goal should be nothing short of having every one of your customers and every one of your networkers become your raving fans. How? By applying the following 10 suggestions:

1. Attract people and business
2. Touch base and help
3. Continually improve
4. Tell your future

5 Share your success

6 Make the most of yourself and your stuff

7 Do the unexpected

8 Your special club

9 Get ahead and stay there

10 Name recognition

1. Attract people and business—be the kind of person people want to be around and want to do business with. Remember, networking is about relationships. And people voluntarily enter into relationships only with people they like. If you want to be liked, you have to be likeable. Ask yourself, "Am I the kind of person I would like to be with?" For many of us, an honest answer to that question is liable to be quite an eye opener. But don't despair. There are some things you can do to increase your chances of being accepted. Dale Carnegie called it *How to Win Friends and Influence People*. Among the most compelling techniques he mentioned are:

○ Remember and use people's names when talking to them.

○ Encourage others to talk, and really listen to them before asking them to listen to you.

○ Praise other people when you can do so sincerely.

○ Don't argue. Instead, discuss issues without implying that anyone who disagrees with you is automatically wrong.

TURN YOUR NETWORKERS AND CUSTOMERS

- Allow people to save face. If someone blunders, focus on solutions, not on the mistake.

- Ask questions or make requests rather than giving orders.

- Praise even small achievements. Encouragement is the best motivator.

- Give a person a good image of themselves to live up to; change behavior by raising self-esteem.

- Make the other person feel happy about doing what you want them to do.

2. Touch base and help—contact all of your customers and your networkers regularly just to touch base, and find out how you can help them. You don't want to make a pest of yourself, but neither can you afford to have people who are important to your success forget about you. A phone call to each of your former clients or customers once a quarter is not unreasonable. Members of your Primary Network should be willing to hear from you even more frequently. Remember, the purpose of your call is to find out what is new with them and to see if you can help them in any way. Do not give the impression that you're just a pesky salesperson looking to push your wares on them. You want to know what you can do for them, not what they can do for you.

3. Continually improve—continually improve your product or service. Good enough is no longer good enough. What you got by with yesterday, you will get buried with tomorrow. You can be sure that your competition, whether they are competing with you directly for customers or trying to make inroads into your network for referrals, will constantly upgrade their offerings. You cannot afford to be left behind.

SUCCESSFUL BUSINESS NETWORKING

The people who will make referrals on your behalf will stick their necks out for you. Neither they nor you can afford to be put in the position of recommending outdated or second class products and services.

4. Tell your future—let your customers and your networkers know about your future plans. Keep your network informed about changes and upgrades that you are planning for the products or services you presently offer. You don't want to give away the store or give your competitors an unfair advantage, but neither can you afford to give the appearance of having a stagnant product line. Also be sure that the upgrades or changes you tell them about really do take place. Once again, your reputation is at stake.

5. Share your success—share your success stories. Let the members of your network and your clients know what the media and other customers have said or are saying about your products and services. If you are fortunate enough to be mentioned in a newspaper or magazine article, buy additional copies or make photocopies and distribute them to the members of your network. People want to be affiliated with winners, and third party testimonials go a long way toward enhancing your esteem in the marketplace.

6. Make the most of yourself and your stuff—teach your networkers how to make the most of your products and services. Don't assume that just because someone is in your network or has purchased your products or services, they are familiar with the best ways to use them. You want your networkers to have their eyes and ears open for opportunities for you. The more they know about your offerings, the greater help they can be. For example, if you are a plumber, you want your customers and networkers to be on the lookout for more than just clogged drains or broken pipes. You want them to know that you can also solve heating and air conditioning problems. Your services could also be valuable to home builders or people adding rooms onto their present house. Give your networkers as many opportunities as possible to pass your name along to prospective customers or clients. Educate them about all of your professional capabilities.

7. Do the unexpected—anybody can do what is expected of them. You can distinguish yourself from your competition by consistently providing more than your customers expect. Develop a reputation as someone who underpromises and overdelivers. We are talking about more than simple customer service. We are talking about doing so much so well that your clients are not only happy with what you have done, but they will go out of their way to refer you to others. Just imagine how much your business could increase if all of your customers were active members of your Primary Network. It can be done, but it is up to you to make them want to support you.

8. Your special club—treat your networkers as if they were members of a special club or group. Give your Primary Networkers and your best customers the feeling that they are indeed special. For example, you might send them a copy of a book or audio tape which you feel they might particularly enjoy. Should you have the opportunity to author articles (or even to write a book), share copies with the members of this special group. You might even consider inviting them to special events, such as a cookout, sporting event, etc. Offer to pay their registration fees for industry-sponsored events such as association meetings, Chamber of Commerce get-togethers and so on. The idea is to make them feel special and to know that they are appreciated by you.

9. Get ahead and stay there—get ahead of the curve, and stay there. Condition yourself to look for and understand trends so that you can be ahead of the competition. Let your customers and networkers know that you are a visionary, and help them to understand how future changes will impact them and their businesses. By helping them to understand the future, you make them more interested and willing to help you, both today and tomorrow.

10. Name recognition—keep your name in front of your clients and your networkers. Use high tech, low tech and no tech to keep people thinking about you. Anything and everything from postcards to lunch meetings to websites and e-mail are fair game in today's competitive business world. The old adage once again bears repeating – "Out of sight, out of mind." You could be a wonderful person with excellent products and have a super-duper special club. But unless your networkers think about you when an opportunity arises to refer you, your efforts will have been for naught. Your present clients and the members of your network are your keys to future business, but only if they remember you. Research has shown that 70 percent of responses come only after people have heard from you a minimum of three times. Just because your first, second or even third attempts to make yourself a household name may have failed, don't give up. Rome wasn't built in a day—neither will your reputation.

Chapter 16

ELEMENTS OF A BROAD-BASED MARKETING CAMPAIGN

Your firm may have the best ideas in the world, own all the latest technology and have great products or services—but it will go out of business if no one hires you. Even well-known firms like Coca-Cola or Proctor and Gamble do not sit back and wait for the phone to ring or for customers to walk in the front door. They became well-known because of their marketing efforts, and they stay successful because of their ability to sell.

ELEMENTS OF MARKETING

Mention the word "marketing" to a group of businesspeople, and you will get a number of responses as to what the word means. Some may think we're talking about brochures or promotional pieces. Others will envision developing and maintaining personal relationships, while still others will talk about the importance of writing articles and giving speeches.

In fact, each of these ideas is correct, but individually each is only part of the answer. Successful companies operate on the realization that developing new business requires a cohesive approach among several different, yet complimentary and mutually supportive elements:

1 Promotion

2 Networking

3 Enticing or Courting

4 Word-of-Mouth Marketing

5 Caring and Nurturing

6 Market Research

1. Promotion—to get business, prospective customers have to know that you are in business. Promotional activities are designed to stimulate inquiries for more information about your services, to generate leads, and to pave the way for additional contacts between you and those who might hire you. Promotional techniques include speeches, seminars, newsletters, articles, public relations programs, and advertising. The objective of promotions is to broadcast your message to (hopefully) a large audience.

2. Networking—we have noted throughout this book that when done correctly, networking is the art of helping others to help you get more business. Networking entails a lot more than asking your

ELEMENTS OF A BROAD-BASED MARKETING CAMPAIGN

friends to give or send you business. Effective networking begins with a desire to help other people. By helping others, you give them a reason to want to help you. The key is to give without expecting a "quid pro quo," because once you start "keeping score" of what other people are doing for you compared to what you have done for them, you begin to get selfish, and selfish people are notoriously poor networkers. Networking is based on a combination of gratitude and trust, and because networking takes time and effort, to be successful at networking requires motivation. You have to let other people know what you do and figure out who knows whom so appropriate introductions can be made. Networking is one of the strongest business development techniques because it has the effect of greatly expanding your sales force and bringing you business.

3. Enticing or Courting—promotion helps you reach groups of prospective customers, and networking gains you introductions. Now you have to focus on enticing or courting specific customers one at a time. Learn as much as you can about the target of your interest, both on an individual and a corporate level. Review trade association directories and Who's Who books for descriptions of key individuals. Browse through annual reports, association publications and 10-K forms for information about the companies you are interested in. You want to find out where this prospect's "hot buttons" are or what "turns them on," which, in turn, will help you to understand the purchasing process. It may help at this stage to put yourself in the client's shoes and think about how you would respond to your firm's marketing approach if you were a buyer. Ask yourself the same kind of questions your customers are asking, and analyze your answers to them—Why should I hire you? (What unique benefits or expertise does your firm offer to help the customer meet his/her needs) Would

I want to work with this person or firm? (How responsive are we, how easy do we make it to do business with us, how friendly, conscientious, etc.). When a client hires you, they are seeking to enter into a relationship with you. Therefore, your marketing process should be viewed as a courtship.

4. Word-of-Mouth Marketing—you can talk all you want about yourself or your firm's capabilities, but when a customer says wonderful things about you, other prospective customers are much more likely to listen. This means that a major component of your marketing efforts should be devoted to keeping your existing clients not just satisfied, but "delighted" with your work. The goal is to have your clients become your fans who proactively seek opportunities to recommend you to their colleagues at other companies who might have need of your services. Word-of-mouth marketing has to be earned and requires effort on your part. The customer expects you to be technically competent, so doing good quality work will leave the customer basically satisfied. But to get your customer to become "part of your marketing team" requires more than technical excellence. The client is not simply buying a product, he is buying peace of mind, trust and reassurance. In effect, a client does not use your products or services, a client experiences them. This means that your marketing efforts must be geared to a client's perceptions, as well as to his expectations. The customer's true needs must be understood and met. Unfortunately, too many firms overlook the importance of being "client centered," and become enthralled with their own technical prowess or intellectual capabilities to the point where we have too often heard otherwise savvy business people lament, "This would be a great job if the customer would get out of the way." An attitude like that is not lost on the customer and would certainly not lead to that customer becoming one of your raving fans.

ELEMENTS OF A BROAD-BASED MARKETING CAMPAIGN

5. Caring and Nurturing—not only do you want your present customers to be so happy with the work you have done for them that they are willing to tell others about you, you also want them to give you additional work themselves. Customers want to feel that you care for them and are not merely using them to beef up your client list. Nor do customers want to be taken for granted. Future business must be earned, yet many companies that have well-structured programs for business development from new customers fail to have an organized plan for getting new business from present customers. This is ironic, since most firms recognize that their best source of new business is from their existing client base. So why do most firms devote most of their time, effort and marketing dollars to new clients rather than to caring for and nurturing existing clients? One reason we often hear is that it is "more fun" to bring in a new client than it is to generate additional business from a present client. Also, most companies tend to more highly value and reward those who bring in new customers versus those who may bring in the same level of new business revenues from present customers. If your firm wants to be fully successful, you will have to take advantage of the opportunities presented by your present customers.

6. Market Research—if you really want to be effective in marketing, you have to know what is going on in the marketplace. The better you know what your customers and prospective customers are thinking and what they want, the more likely you will be able to convince them that you can meet their needs. If you want to know what your clients are thinking, ask them. But ask them in a systematic and organized way—and then listen and respond to what they have to say. Successful firms invest in market intelligence rather than basing their business development activities on guesses or assumptions.

They also have mechanisms in place to share the data collected with the right people within their firms. Market research done properly is about more than just gathering data. It is also necessary to use the data.

MARKETING METHODS

Regardless of the business, profession or industry you serve, you have an opportunity to be quite creative in your marketing approaches. However, very few companies are innovative in their techniques. In fact, most firms, especially professional service firms, do not market themselves very well at all. Perhaps this is due to the perception that as "professionals" it is somehow demeaning to think of themselves as "marketers" or "salespeople." Many firms have traditionally used terms like business development, practice development or relationship building to somehow hide the fact that they were engaged in marketing initiatives. Regardless of what they may call it (a rose by any other name...), successful firms have learned to utilize a variety of techniques to bring in new business. Among the more common methods are:

1 Personal Contacts

2 Referrals

3 Speeches/Training Programs

4 Articles and Books

5 Research

ELEMENTS OF A BROAD-BASED MARKETING CAMPAIGN

6 Public Relations

7 Cold Calls

8 Advertising

1. Personal Contacts—chances are that you know or can be introduced to people who are in need of your products and services. In fact, personal connections are the favored method to find new customers, and for potential customers to find you. With the innumerable possible customers out there and their basic lack of knowledge about who does what you do, coupled with the limited marketing budgets of most companies, it's no wonder that personal contacts are the best way for sellers and buyers to find out if they are right for each other.

As noted previously, the most profitable source of new business comes from having a good relationship with your existing clients who can give you additional business. The goal should be to develop an ever closer relationship with your clients. There are three good reasons for doing so:

○ The costs of prospecting are usually lower than the costs for developing new clients.

○ Trust and confidence are key components in selling, so if you have already developed a relationship, the battle is partially won.

○ Clients are usually less sensitive about costs or fees for follow-up work than for initial purchases.

So how can you develop better relationships with your customers? Well, you can:

- Increase the amount and frequency of contact with your customers by phoning often, visiting regularly, introducing other members of your staff to your customers, and, to the greatest extent possible, getting additional people from the customer's organization involved in your project.

- Improve your personal relationship with the client by remembering the customer's family, their names and important dates, by inviting the customer to social and sporting events, and by making it easy for customers to get in touch with you.

- Send the customer copies of articles of interest, offer to put on a seminar or training program for this customer's staff members, and/or offer to attend the customer's company meetings.

As more firms come to realize the importance of their existing client base, some are assigning a senior level executive to serve as a "client relationship manager." Rather than just being concerned about a single project, a relationship manager is concerned about a particular client and all of the services provided or offered to that client.

2. Referrals—there are any number of potential sources for referrals; unfortunately, too many companies do not tap into these sources very effectively. Referrals are often available from within your own firm, especially if your firm is large and offers multiple services or works in several industries. At first glance, this type of referral would seem to be obvious. In reality, however, cross-referral and cross-selling are more matters of wishful thinking in most firms than they are large revenue generators. Some of the reasons for this will be discussed later in this book.

ELEMENTS OF A BROAD-BASED MARKETING CAMPAIGN

Referrals can come from other firms providing services to the client. Many companies have established formal and informal networks with consulting, accounting, law, public relations and advertising firms for the express purpose of referring business back and forth in non-competing practice areas. In addition, don't overlook your own firm's outside advisors who might be able to refer your firm to some of their other clients.

Your firm's board of directors can also be a source of referrals. Many firms have business executives, academics and others who often have their own extensive networks of people, some of whom could potentially become your clients.

Likewise, your customers can provide you with referrals. In some cases your clients' CEO or other senior officers may serve on the boards of other companies and can share information about you with their colleagues from other industries. Remember though, if they are not satisfied with your work, they will also let that be known.

Active membership and participation in trade and professional associations which represent your business area or industry can result in referrals. Your firm should also be active and visible in the associations where your customers and prospective customers are members. Many of these groups have their own referral systems or publish "buyer's guides" to help their members locate needed goods and services.

And don't forget about suppliers as sources of referrals. Some companies have relationships with computer hardware and software manufacturers which generate a number of opportunities. Depending on the nature of your business, there may be opportunities for you as well with such diverse entities as banks, insurance companies, construction firms, logistics and warehouse equipment manufacturers, shipping and transportation companies, etc.

3. Speeches/Training Programs—presenting at seminars can help you position yourself as an expert, enhances your visibility and allows you to interact with prospective customers in a professional setting. The key, of course, is to follow up after the conference (assuming, of course, that you did a good job with your presentation). If you can get a copy of the registration list from the seminar sponsor, your follow up is made easier. If not, it is up to you to collect business cards by directly asking for them, or by offering to send something (an article, a copy of your speech, etc.) to those who turn in their business card.

An alternative is for your firm to host its own seminars. By doing so you get to control the attendance and the agenda and to present yourself and your firm as "experts" on the topic(s) of your choice. To be successful, however, the seminar must be of value to those you invite and have something new to say. Some firms have been so successful hosting seminars and training programs, that not only are they able to use them to introduce their new products and services, but their seminars and training programs have actually become profit centers for the firms.

4. Articles and Books—being a published author provides you with heightened credibility and keeps your name in front of prospective clients even when you are not there. The best and most effective articles are those which position you as a "thought leader" and which make the reader want to get in touch with you. Some larger firms even publish and distribute their own high quality magazines which they feel are helpful in their prospecting efforts—they give the marketing team something to talk about, and they differentiate the firm from its competition.

Articles can be reprinted and handed out at speeches and conferences; reprints can also be mailed to your present and prospective clients, and they can be sent to people who call you to ask if you have expertise in a particular area. Well done articles can be an effective marketing tool for many years.

So if articles and books (though books may not be read by as large an audience as an article, they allow you to say that your firm "wrote the book on the subject") are so valuable, why don't more businesses use them? The answer lies in the fact that writing takes time and discipline. Successful companies have learned, however, that the effort is more than justified by the rewards.

5. Research—information and data provide the basis for seminars, articles and books. The depth and breadth of the research can vary from major global studies to relatively simple opinion surveys of what a particular group thinks about a given subject. Research does not have to cost a lot of money to generate a lot of publicity for your firm. There is usually a great deal of interest about business-related issues, so the business media is frequently looking for material.

Research conducted on topics of interest to your customers increases your value to them by helping them and you to stay abreast of emerging trends in their industry. Try to provide your customers with information they cannot readily get from other sources. You want to be able to distinguish yourself as a resource your customer needs. The information collected could be technical or professional in nature (new products, standards, techniques, etc.) or it could be somewhat more general: such as a survey of industry leaders on their most pressing problems, the solutions they have attempted and a ranking of the effectiveness of the various techniques. While research of this type may not result in "breakthrough thinking," it is valuable to your customers because it can help them compare their company to their competition and may save them time and money.

Some firms have successfully enticed trade or professional associations to "partner" with them on research projects. In some cases the association may even underwrite or sponsor the financing of the research, but just getting the association's name affiliated with yours lends an aura of credibility to your firm.

Conducting research for use in articles and books can also be used as a technique for getting you in front of prospective clients. Senior executives who may not otherwise be accessible to you for a "sales call" may be willing to meet with you if the purpose of your visit (or phone call) is to interview them as part of your research for an article. Be honest, however, if you do get to meet them or talk to them. Limit the discussion to the gathering of research information. Don't try to turn the opportunity into a sales call unless the other person invites you to do so by asking you for specific information about your firm. For now, it is simply enough to have had the chance to meet or talk. And always offer to send the executive a copy of your article or relevant portions of the manuscript prior to submitting it for publication so he can review any quotes attributed to him for accuracy. This gives you a second opportunity to establish contact. You have a third chance to get your name in front of the prospective client when you send him a copy or reprint of the published article or book. The more familiar your name is to the prospect, the greater the chance you have of winding up with a new client.

ELEMENTS OF A BROAD-BASED MARKETING CAMPAIGN

6. Public Relations—because PR is an indirect approach to generating publicity, the efforts may not generate any results for a while. But because references to your firm and its capabilities are presented in ways that do not appear to be blatant or self-serving, the impact on prospective clients can be very effective. Bear in mind, however, that just because you send out press releases, those to whom they are sent are under no obligation to use them. Many, if not most, press releases find their way into trash cans. And if your "news" is picked up for use in an article or news story, there is no guarantee that it will necessarily always be used in a favorable context. You do not control the agenda or thrust of the story. However, a well-planned, proactive public relations effort can help to position you as a resource for journalists who may respond by placing you in a more favorable light in their articles.

Public relations efforts can and should be a key component of your marketing efforts. As such, PR requires time and effort and is worth paying attention to. But far too many firms do not do a very good job managing or monitoring the quality and/or efficacy of their PR campaign. In fact, many firms fail to see public relations activities as a campaign, but rather tend to think of PR more in terms of either "damage control" (i.e., trying to put a positive "spin" on a negative occurrence) or as a means of announcing a special event. In today's competitive marketplace, PR cannot be thought of as something you or a member of your staff does in his or her spare time in addition to their other duties.

7. Cold Calls—the thought of "pounding the pavement" and "banging on doors" in an attempt to sell your services is enough to give some people apoplexy. Cold calling has traditionally been thought of in terms of selling products like encyclopedias, vacuum cleaners and magazine subscriptions door to door, not as a means of marketing professional services. Nevertheless, more and more frequently we run into professional service firms who utilize professional salespeople and even telemarketers to set up appointments for the firm's executives to get in front of prospective clients. We are not intending to conjure up images of a van full of nattily attired and carefully groomed executive type people set loose in an industrial or business park with order books in hand, methodically ringing doorbells. But where careful prior research has been done on the prospective client, then a carefully crafted call to arrange a customized, face-to-face meeting can be quite successful.

8. Advertising—opponents argue that advertising is an expensive means of reaching a large audience that does not buy services out of a magazine or from a telephone number on the television screen. Proponents counter that such activities afford the firm increased visibility and enhanced relationships with clients and potential clients.

If you do decide to engage in an advertising campaign, make sure you do some careful advance planning and research to ensure that your ads are placed where your customers and prospects are most likely to see them. Find out what magazines, newspapers and trade publications your target audience reads. Understand specifically who you want to reach and what message you want to leave them with after seeing your ad. How will you get them to take the time to look at, much less read, watch or listen to your ad? Some firms use humor, others play on the concerns of their target audience, others provide an answer to a commonly asked question, and still others rely on captivating graphics to grab attention.

ELEMENTS OF A BROAD-BASED MARKETING CAMPAIGN

Also when thinking about the use of advertising as a marketing technique, bear in mind the old, but nonetheless very true, adage, "repetition makes reputation." A one-time shot at advertising is not an efficient use of your money, even if you do mail out copies of the ad or the whole magazine to your target audience after the ad appears. With advertising, as with PR, be prepared to hang in there for the long term.

In addition to the marketing methods listed above, there are other activities worth considering, such as becoming involved in community and civic groups; cultivating clients at social or sporting events; direct mail campaigns; and publishing and distributing newsletters.

Of course, any and all of these techniques can work and will work sometimes. We have all heard stories of contracts brought in as a result of a golf match or ball game. Community involvement can help you meet people, and as long as your newsletter can avoid becoming simply a repository for generic information, your target audience may find it interesting enough to read.

Different marketing methods are important to have, but there must be a coordinated, planned approach to using them which is aimed at a targeted audience, if your marketing efforts are really going to be successful.

STRATEGIC POSITIONING OPTIONS

Deciding how your firm is going to compete is an important prelude to designing your marketing plan. How your firm is positioned determines to a large extent who you will compete against and even what you are going to market. There are several different strategic positioning options. These include:

- The focus of the firm, i.e., the firm concentrates on the services or products it will offer, the customers it will target, and/or the geographic market it serves.

- The firm can use its own image as a sales tool.

- The firm can compete on the basis of providing superior quality and consistency.

- The firm can market its ability to provide other services or products in addition to its core services.

- A low price relative to the value of services offered is another competitive position the firm can take.

Your firm's approach to positioning must be an integral component of both your strategic and marketing plans. We have found examples of successful firms which compete on the basis of each of the options listed above. Consistency of message is the key.

MARKETING ADVICE

The following is a compilation of advice we have gleaned in our years as consultants and trainers.

ELEMENTS OF A BROAD-BASED MARKETING CAMPAIGN

○ **Walk the talk**—be and act like you are what you say you are. Establish the values of your firm, live up to those values, and instill them in your staff and in your networkers.

○ **Proper positioning**—determine the strategic positioning of your firm in accordance with your firm's values, and build your marketing efforts around that positioning.

○ **Credible claims**—be honest and believable in stating what your firm can and cannot do. A good rule of thumb is to treat every sale or project as though it were going to appear in tomorrow's newspaper, or as though you were going to have to defend your position in court.

○ **Consistent message**—make sure all your supporting materials convey the image you want to have for your firm.

○ **Establish an identity**—"Build a better mousetrap, and the world will beat a path to your door," is the old saying, but it only applies to you if the world knows you built it and where you live. Customers have to know that you exist before they can hire you. Develop and promote a consistent identity. Also make sure that the logo, typeface, etc. is similar on all of your promotional materials rather than looking like you just threw a variety of pieces together.

○ **Develop relationships**, **don't sell products**—trust is built on relationships, not on products. An analogy to keep in mind in your marketing efforts is: "Tell the customer about the lawn he can have, not about your grass seed." Help the client envision the benefits he will derive rather than focusing on the product you're selling.

SUCCESSFUL BUSINESS NETWORKING

○ **Listen, don't tell**—the customer wants you to solve his problem and to understand his concerns. You can do this only by listening to the customer rather than talking about your pre-packaged solutions or pre-conceived notions.

○ **Customer testimonials work**—it is one thing to say good things about yourself; however, they are much more believable and effective when someone else says them. Granted, many of your customers may not want you to use their names, but you won't know unless you ask.

○ **Establish and follow a marketing/sales sequence**—develop an understanding of the full extent of the customer's need/problem. Establish and help the customer see the full cost of not meeting the need/problem. Demonstrate your ability to meet the need/problem. Establish and help the client see the cost/payoff equation.

○ **Manage your time and your staff's time**—monitor how you and your staff use time when not working on client projects. Make sure you all use this time in ways that will benefit your firm, such as marketing-related activities or personal and professional development initiatives.

10 TECHNIQUES TO GET MORE BUSINESS

1 Determine who you want as customers and contact them. Repeatedly send them useful information about their industry's issues or their specific problems, along with a personalized letter.

ELEMENTS OF A BROAD-BASED MARKETING CAMPAIGN

2   Do excellent work. Exceed the expectations of your current clients and encourage them to refer you to their customers, suppliers and corporate friends.

3   Develop case histories of your success stories. Identify the problem you solved or the need you met and how you did it, and send these case histories for use as articles or sidebars to editors of publications read by your target audience.

4   Be visible. Write articles, give speeches, get interviewed, teach courses, attend and participate in trade and professional associations, etc.

5   Stay in touch with prospective, former and present customers. Publish a newsletter filled with genuinely valuable information and helpful analysis. Strive for four to six issues a year to keep your name in front of your customers.

6   Develop and use networks. Participate in professional, service, social and community organizations. Get involved and become known in associations representing your trade or profession and in associations that your customers or prospects are members of—they can be a good source of referrals, and other members might become part or your Primary Network.

7   Conduct a self-assessment. Analyze your firm's strengths and weaknesses compared to those of your top competitors. Determine how you can capitalize on your strengths and overcome your weaknesses so you will be able and ready to answer questions your prospective clients might raise.

8   Differentiate your firm. Brainstorm with your staff, customers, suppliers, friends, etc. and try to develop a list of "50 Reasons

Why We Should Be the Company You Hire." Pay particular attention to everything that makes you different from your competition, and decide how to capitalize on these differences.

9 Use advertising if you can afford to. It's expensive, but advertising works if you want to reach large groups of people repeatedly. Remember, "repetition makes reputation"—advertising is not as cost-effective as a one-time event.

10 Budget for marketing. Business development requires time, effort, money and management—successful firms budget and plan accordingly.

SOME FINAL THOUGHTS ABOUT MARKETING

There is no direct evidence that having a high-quality brochure outlining your firm's capabilities will gain you additional business, but when all of your competitors do have them, not having one can hurt you.

Regardless of the size of your firm, you can't be all things to all people. It is necessary to define the market(s) you are going to concentrate on. Depending on the nature of your practice, you may define it by industry or by service offering, but remember, customers want to hire specialists. After targeting a select group of companies to contact, research each specific company prior to contacting them directly. The more individualized you can make the sales contact, the greater your chances of making the sale. Remember, marketing, sales and project work are all team efforts, and it is important from the outset to coordinate these teams and to assign responsibilities for management.

ELEMENTS OF A BROAD-BASED MARKETING CAMPAIGN

Within your defined market everybody can be viewed as a prospective customer, but some deserve special targeting for proactive sales efforts. Targets are usually selected based on: size (the company is the size that you are best able to serve); industry (where you have the greatest experience, or an industry you want to gain experience in); ability to pay (you may be altruistic by nature, but remember, you still have a business to run); need/problem of the client is a match with your capabilities; management level (market to people who actually hire and/or work with you, not to the CEO just because it boosts your ego).

The primary purpose of promotional efforts is to generate interest in and an awareness of your company among prospective customers. Promotional activities may not result in direct sales, but they are used to obtain referrals, to gain intelligence about companies that might be interested in your services, to be asked to come in to a company to make a proposal, and to be introduced to company decision makers. Among the more common promotional activities are: making speeches at meetings where prospective customers are in attendance; writing articles to appear in publications read by clients; letting people know about you and your firm; and attending group meetings such as professional societies, trade associations, community groups, social settings, church activities, school groups, etc. In addition, compiling, allocating and managing the sales tools available to you must be taken into consideration as part of your firm's marketing plan. Sales tools include telephones, business cards, letters, testimonials, brochures/surveys/reprints and lists of qualifications.

Chapter 17

60 PLUS SECRETS OF MARKETING

In marketing, the recipe for success includes a variety of ingredients, including: developing and training your networkers, involving your customers and prospective customers, staying aware of (and hopefully ahead of) your competition, constant innovation, and taking advantage of cross-selling opportunities. Here are five dozen marketing concepts, techniques and strategies that really work:

1. Position your services, products, expertise and your firm. How do you want your prospective clients to think about your firm and its services? What does that prospect think about your competition? How can you break through the idea that "you're all the same" and

differentiate your firm in the mind of the buyer? How can you establish yourself as the "first one that comes to mind" when prospective customers think about firms in your line of work? There are many books and articles available about positioning—find them, read them, and put their ideas to work.

2   Involve the customer. Use every opportunity to stay in touch with your customers. Present customers are your best source for uncovering and finding what your prospective customers are likely to need. Use the information to refine your marketing program. Every time you talk to a customer, it is a fact-finding and marketing opportunity. Also, don't forget to survey customers at the conclusion of each project or sale. Not only will the results help you to refine your future marketing activities, but they may uncover opportunities for add-on services with the customer who is responding to the survey.

3   Use your firm's best-selling services/products to help sell other activities. Don't be afraid to "ride the coattail" of your most popular services. If you sell flowers, use your expertise to sell balloons, cards, party favors, or even to sell advice on party planning. If you offer computer systems, use it to open the door for consulting services. Think about the broader needs of the customer from the customer's perspective.

4   Understand the difference between marketing and sales. Marketing is primarily foundational in nature. It includes the work you do to understand customers and markets, as well as matching services and products to identified needs. Sales is the implementation of marketing initiatives. Both marketing and sales are crucial to success.

60 PLUS SECRETS OF MARKETING 263

5 Constantly innovate and develop your services and products so they provide benefits to clients. You can't afford to sit still. In the words of Will Rogers, "Even if you're on the right track, you can get run over when the train comes through." If you don't take the time to improve your offerings, your competitors will run you over. Real profits lie in improving and customizing; thus your hardest work and highest costs should be put into developing your offerings and establishing them in the marketplace.

6 Track everything you do and analyze what you've done. Learn from both your successes and your failures. Determine what types of marketing activities and materials work best for your firm and your target market. Find out how prospective customers first heard about your firm.

7 Practice client-savvy, client-driven—not product- or service-driven—marketing. Build your marketing and sales efforts around what your clients need, not around what you have to sell.

8 Identify client needs through market research. Use feedback mechanisms and meetings to identify issues of concern to your customers. If you don't have market research capabilities in house, contract out. Sometimes you can even get free or low cost help from your local college or university by offering to become a case study for one of their marketing courses.

9 Provide exceptional service and value. Client loyalty is built on value and service, not on price. Delivering more than the client expected turns the client into an advocate and potentially gets them into your active network.

10 Know who your customers are. Understand and target your marketing efforts at the right people at the right level in the right companies, i.e., those who actually buy your products and services. A fancy campaign aimed at the CEO might make you feel good, but it won't result in any business if someone else makes the decision whether or not to hire you. Develop profiles of your targeted customers and determine their interests, needs, purchasing process, and key decision makers.

11 Never lose a customer or proposal without finding out why. Turn negative events into learning experiences so you can do better in the future. Don't be afraid to ask "Why." You may learn some very helpful information about your firm and/or your competition.

12 Monitor and understand the trends impacting your firm, your industry, and your customers. Many firms at least try to keep abreast of changes and trends that their clients are confronting. Successful firms also realize that the entire industry itself may be undergoing change. Participate in organizations and associations where you can share information and learn from your peers.

13 Integrate your services and products into a single marketing function. Let the marketplace see all of the services your firm has to offer. A unified marketing approach also helps your staff with cross-selling.

14 Cultivate prior clients. Don't forget about past clients. They may have new needs you can meet, so you may be able to generate new business from them directly. By keeping your name in front of them, they are more likely to think of you when they are asked for referrals.

60 PLUS SECRETS OF MARKETING

15 Market relationships rather than sell projects. Invest in the time and technology to build up-to-date databases which permit you to identify and qualify prospective customers and then focus and target your marketing efforts on understanding and meeting the specific needs of each individual prospect.

16 Keep an eye on the calendar. Marketing campaigns require paying attention to timing. Understanding your customer's budgeting cycle lets you time your proposal to arrive just before the process begins. Timing is also important in following up when you said you would.

17 Target your mailings. Mailings can keep your name in front of prospects and customers, but the materials they receive must be relevant to them or you will be sending the wrong message. Keep your mailing lists up to date as well. Mail sent to the wrong person or wrong address is unprofessional.

18 Create awareness through sponsorship. You can sponsor or host cocktail parties or other activities at a trade association meeting where your clients and prospects will be in attendance. Or how about an exhibit or booth at a trade show? The key is to build name recognition.

19 Write articles highlighting success stories about your services. Develop articles for both trade publications and for dissemination to the general public media. Don't assume that other staff members in your firm are aware of what you're doing. Keep them, as well as your customers and prospects, informed.

20 Plan the timing of your mail delivery. Send mail on Monday or Tuesday so it arrives later in the week when there is traditionally less volume. Your mailing has a better chance of being read if there is less competition.

21 Develop a list of all the services and products offered by your firm. Ask each person in your company to contribute to a master list of everything your firm offers. Such a list is invaluable in writing marketing copy and for identifying cross-selling opportunities.

22 Listen when customers call to help identify needs. Determine what people are asking for by paying attention to and tracking incoming calls. If you find that a significant number are inquiries about a specific product or service, consider expanding your visibility in that area if it is something you presently offer, or explore the feasibility of developing a capability in that area if you don't presently offer it.

23 Remind yourself and your staff what business you're really in. Generally speaking, no matter what products or services you offer, you are in the business of helping customers solve problems. This implies an attitude of service—the customer really does come first.

24 Use focus groups and follow up. Focus groups can be very helpful in developing new approaches, techniques, practices, etc. If you use focus groups, however, don't forget to follow up with the participants regarding the outcome. They want to feel that they made a difference, and using them shows a greater sense of commitment to your firm.

60 PLUS SECRETS OF MARKETING

267

25 Prepare a written plan for every marketing initiative. A plan keeps you from simply focusing on the easy stuff. Putting it in writing lets all of your staff know what you're trying to do and how they can help.

26 Commit to client satisfaction. Position your firm as a quality provider dedicated to keeping clients happy. Remember that a satisfied client is your best form of advertisement and can turn your customer into an adjunct to your sales force.

27 Bundle your offerings. Develop tailored bundles or packages of services you can offer to meet the specific needs of individual customers. Let them know all the ways you can be of service to them.

28 Add value rather than cut the price. It's a competitive market, and you will be pressured to lower your prices. Don't do it. Instead, demonstrate all the extra benefits and value the customer will receive from your efforts in excess of the proposed costs. If the customer still says the price is too high, offer to narrow the scope of the project to bring the cost down rather than discounting your prices.

29 Know your competition. Take time to find out as much as you can about your competition, including products, practice areas, strategy, objectives, pricing, etc. See how they service their customers and what they are developing as new markets.

30 Let your customers know what's in it for them. Customers want to know what they are going to get for their money. They may think you're wonderful, but they still want to know: "What's in it for me?" Develop a market plan from the perspective of the customer.

SUCCESSFUL BUSINESS NETWORKING

31 Establish realistic and measurable goals. Impossible goals and unrealistic expectations will kill your best marketers. Don't do that. Make goals measurable so you can track success.

32 Communicate value and service. If you're good, let the world know. If you don't tell your story, no one else will do it for you.

33 Set time limits for your proposals to remain in effect. Let prospects know that the terms, conditions and prices quoted in your proposal will remain in effect for a certain period of time (usually 30 days). You may prevent an awkward situation if prospective customers try to hold you to old prices.

34 Don't underprice. Your price should reflect the quality of your products and services. Many of your customers may adhere to the adage, "You get what you pay for."

35 Cross-sell. Never miss an opportunity to let a customer know all of the capabilities of your firm. Cross-selling is a low-cost way to expand your business and to build customer loyalty.

36 Do your selling in the cover letter. Target the letter to the specific audience, and let them know how you are going to meet their needs as well as the benefits they will derive. Don't write an "enclosed is a brochure" style form letter.

37 Use testimonials. Using testimonials from satisfied customers adds interest and credibility to your marketing efforts.

38 Make it easy for your customers to reach you. Include your firm's telephone numbers, fax numbers and e-mail addresses on all correspondence. Don't assume people have your data on file.

60 PLUS SECRETS OF MARKETING 269

39 Allocate resources properly. Line up your resources before beginning a marketing initiative. If you sign up customers and can't service them properly or in a timely manner, you will not only lose them, you will turn them into detractors.

40 Establish a corporate identity. Strong and consistent graphics are essential to your firm's success. You need pieces that contribute to building a strong, recognizable identity for your firm in the marketplace.

41 Create events. If you or one of your staff writes a book, create a media-covered book signing event. Sponsor symposia, workshops, breakfast, lunch or dinner meetings. Bring in outside speakers and invite customers to attend a presentation/reception. Create opportunities for people to talk about your firm.

42 Use a postscript (P.S.). People will read it. Make sure it has a powerful selling message.

43 Develop and distribute a publication. Newsletters, magazines, journals, etc., if done properly, can be excellent marketing tools. Include articles by people outside of your firm to enhance credibility.

44 Send fax reminders of your events. They serve as last-minute marketing opportunities, and you can generally increase attendance at your events.

45 Acknowledge every client contact. Thank you notes are the least expensive form of public relations between you and your clients. Accept no excuses or delays in acknowledging every meeting or contact with a customer or prospect.

46 Constantly measure your success. Track every marketing initiative and sale. Build a database of what works and what doesn't work based on facts, not suppositions.

47 Cut mailing costs while adding value. Tailor your mailings to the needs of each prospect or customer rather than sending out large packets of generic information.

48 Say thank you. It never hurts to keep thanking your customers. Let them know that you appreciate their business, and they are more likely to want to do business with you again.

49 Use newsletters as marketing and sales tools. Prepare a newsletter that's full of good and useful information. Within the body of the newsletter, position columns that sell your services and products. Be sure that your sales pitch is germane to the article in which it is positioned.

50 Set up a fax-on-demand system. Offer a fax-on-demand and/or an on-line system to make it easy for clients to obtain information about your firm. Include articles written by your staff members. Track requests for information so you can follow up.

51 Concentrate on your areas of success. Find your niche and fill it. Stake out your position so strongly that others can't compete effectively. You can't do it all, so focus on what you do most successfully.

52 Take care of you staff. Respect and treat your staff well, and they will treat your clients with respect. Don't just focus on your professional level staff. Remember that those who answer the telephone and support you will also have contact with customers.

60 PLUS SECRETS OF MARKETING

271

53 Make it easy for customers to provide feedback. Solicit feedback during and after each sale or project. Let the customer know that you listen to and act on his suggestions.

54 Invest in customer service training. Provide training for all those who will have contact with customers. Your investment will more than pay for itself in good customer relationships, repeat business and referrals.

55 Stay close to your customers. Never take a client for granted, especially a long-term customer. Make a commitment to constantly strengthen relationships. Do research to keep in touch with the needs of your customers.

56 Reward for repeat business. Don't fall into the trap of rewarding those who bring in new clients while offering less or no incentives to those who develop repeat business from present clients. Encourage your staff to be alert for additional ways your firm can help the client.

57 Investigate and evaluate joint ventures before jumping into them. Joint marketing initiatives (such as co-sponsored seminars, etc.) between your firm and another firm or vendor can be effective, but do your homework in advance. Test the reputation of the other firm with the target audience for the program. Have any contracts reviewed by legal counsel before signing. Agree in advance on mailing lists and ownership of those lists, etc.

58 Expand your reach through affiliations. Formal and informal networking groups can introduce you to new opportunities.

SUCCESSFUL BUSINESS NETWORKING

59 Respond promptly to complaints. You can often turn a negative experience around by quickly responding to a complaint and involving the unsatisfied client in developing a resolution.

60 Reach for the sky sometimes. Once in a while set an unrealistic goal. You may be surprised at how close you can come to achieving it.

61 Maintain high standards and ethics. Quality is not enough. Customers must be able to trust you and the people who work for you. If you utilize associates or sub-contractors, select people with the same ethical standards as yours.

62 Build strong relationships with clients. A client is worth more than an individual project. Treat them as though your entire future depends on keeping them happy—it does.

63 Delegate. Just because you're the boss doesn't mean you have to do or personally oversee everything. You'll drive yourself crazy if you do, and you'll stifle the development of others.

64 Always give more than the customer expects. In today's competitive marketplace, simply meeting expectations is not sufficient. If you promised 10 benefits, give them more.

65 Bear in mind that low-cost suppliers don't always deliver the best value. Don't be "penny wise and pound foolish" when hiring outside resources such as public relations counsel, printers, etc. Your firm's image is at stake.

66 Customers buy solutions, not products. Market and sell benefits and solutions. Focus on relationships, not projects.

67 Deliver more than you promise. Remember, we offered you 60 tips, but delivered a bonus. There are more than 65 tips presented here.

Part VII

OPEN NEW MARKETS

SECRET 6:

UNITED WE STAND,
DIVERSIFIED WE CONQUER

REFERRAL GROUPS, CHAMBERS AND ASSOCIATIONS

When we talk about diversifying your networks, you have many choices. The three easiest and most direct are:

- Referral Groups
- Chambers of Commerce
- Professional and Trade Associations

All three of these groups are similar in purpose yet different in function. That is why it is important for you to belong to all of them. As a local business you want the people and professionals in your community to know that you are involved in the local community. This is especially important if the majority of your business comes from local support.

SUCCESSFUL BUSINESS NETWORKING

However, even if the majority of business comes from outside your local area, it is important to know who the local players are and for them to know you. You never know who knows whom.

REFERRAL GROUPS

If you want to make more money through referrals, join a referral group. It really is that simple. I'm not saying it is going to be easy, but the decision to join one is a "No Brainer." I have been intimately involved with a business referral group for quite a few years. I cannot refer someone or something with my blessing unless I have a direct experience or relationship with that person or organization. The Business Network International (BNI) is the biggest and most successful business referral organization in the world. I can recommend them highly because I have seen how their chapters run, and I believe in their structure and corporate philosophy. I have met with the founder, Dr. Ivan Misner, and can say that he is a man who is 100 percent focused on making a positive difference in the business community. I am not saying anything negative about any other referral organization. In fact, I have never been to another referral organization's meetings, so I have no knowledge of how they're run. If you've never been to a BNI meeting or if you've never heard of them, call the main office at 1-800-825-8286; look them up on the Web at www.bni.com; or write to BNI at 199 Monte Vista Avenue, Suite 6, San Dimas, CA 91773-3080.

The purpose of these referral groups is for you to help grow your business through a formalized and structured word-of-mouth marketing strategy. There is only one person per profession allowed in a

REFERRAL GROUPS, CHAMBERS AND ASSOCIATIONS

chapter. This means that if you join as the life insurance agent, there can be no other life insurance agent in the group because you are trying to build relationships and, therefore, loyalties with people in the group. When you join one of these chapters you must be committed to working the organization. That means you must go to the weekly meetings regularly. Most of them have attendance policies. You should also get to know the members in the group personally. Get together for breakfast, lunch, dinner or coffee. Sit and talk. Find out about each other's business, families, interests, goals, etc. You are going to want to build an extensive bio on them, as we discussed earlier. As you get to know the people in your referral group better, you will feel more confident referring them to others. That is what these groups are all about: you referring business to them and they referring business to you.

That is what this whole book is about. We have shown you how to build your own extensive network of people to help build your business. These business referral groups are made up of like-minded people. We cannot recommend a better way to directly increase your business than to get involved wholeheartedly in one of these groups.

CHAMBERS OF COMMERCE

If you are not a member of your local chamber of commerce, you are making a mistake and missing out on a lot of business. I know some of you are ex-chamber members. You didn't rejoin because you felt it wasn't worthwhile. Let me list the top 10 reasons people don't rejoin chambers.

Top 10 Reasons for Not Rejoining the Chamber (None of which are valid):

1 "I got no business."

2 "The one here is more a political organization than a business one."

3 "There are too many cliques."

4 "I joined and ended up volunteering my time for all these events that had nothing to do with increasing my business."

5 "It's for top executives of companies only, not the small business owner."

6 "They don't work."

7 "I'm too busy."

8 "I can't afford it."

9 "I felt like and outsider."

10 "Everything they do for you just costs more money."

Do any of these sound familiar to you? Believe me, we've heard them all. We've consulted with many chambers on how to increase their retention rate and give greater value to their members. Some chambers need a lot of work, and some are doing a great job. Yet, some members of every chamber say, "Chambers don't work." Usually these are the people who are not involved in any of the committees and don't network correctly at the mixers.

I'll let you in on a secret: You're right, chambers don't WORK. You know why? They're not supposed to WORK. YOU ARE! People tell me all the time that they joined the chamber to increase their business, but it didn't work. It's not the chamber's job to create more business for you. It is

REFERRAL GROUPS, CHAMBERS AND ASSOCIATIONS

their job to provide opportunities for you to meet other business professionals in the area so you can create more business for yourself.

The Chamber of Commerce has many different functions. Here are a few of them:

1 Legislative Lobbying

2 Business Education Programs

3 Local Government Liaison

4 Health Benefit Programs

5 Tourist Information Center

6 Job Placement Services

7 Free Business Counseling

8 A Network of Business Contacts

9 Referrals to Prospective Clients

10 Leadership Training

11 Business Workshops

12 Marketing and Sponsorship Opportunities

13 International Trade Opportunities

14 Informative Speakers

15 Networking Opportunities

16 Community Involvement

17 Resource Information

SUCCESSFUL BUSINESS NETWORKING

As you can see, the local chambers have a number of responsibilities; but we'll say it again, it is not their job to build your business. It is their job to provide various opportunities for you to build your business. What are some of those opportunities, you ask?

1 Networking Mixers

2 Business Expos

3 Advertising space in their newsletter or publications

4 Volunteer positions

5 Project committees

Often the movers and shakers in the community will be involved in chamber committees. Do they end up doing some business with each other? Yes. Are they doing business with each other because they are on these committees? No. They are doing business with each other because they have built relationships through their involvement in these committees. The time they spend together helping the chamber allows them to get to know each other better. As they get to know, trust and like each other more, they end up doing business and referring business to each other. This is what networking is all about.

What are the five biggest mistakes people make when joining a chamber?

1 Believing the chamber will be their client

2 Being pushy

3 Not getting involved

REFERRAL GROUPS, CHAMBERS AND ASSOCIATIONS

4 Not asking for help

5 Not getting to know the staff

1. Believing the chamber will be their client—believing that by joining the chamber, the chamber itself will become a client is a very unrealistic goal. The chamber is a very connected organization. After all, they know all of the businesspeople in the community. Don't think that by becoming a member you will instantly get business from the chamber. You may down the road when they get to know you better. It's the same old story. If you want to get a big client, then you're going to have to get to know the right people. This not only means joining, but getting involved and learning to network.

2. Being pushy—pushy people are people who are out for themselves and unwilling to help others. People want to help others who they feel want to help them. If you join the chamber expecting that other chamber members and staff are going to instantly support your business, you're wrong. Joining has made you part of the same organization. That creates an instant bond between you and all chamber members— not a strong bond, but a bond. You now need to develop that bond. If you want these members to support you, then you must first support them. Go to their place of business, let them know you are also a chamber member and that you believe in supporting other chamber members. Let them know you would like to get together to learn more about their business to see if you can send more business their way. Then let them know that you would really appreciate their support if the need for your product or service arises in the future. Don't push, build relationships.

3. Not getting involved—the biggest mistake people make when they join the chamber is not getting involved in any of the committees, groups or boards. By getting involved, you are showing people that you are a giving person. The most valuable commodity we have is our time. If you choose to allocate time to some group, organization or activity, it means a lot. Get involved and show people your professionalism at any task you take on. This will directly reflect on everything else you do. When you are on a committee, and every time you have a job to do you do it well, on time, and with your own flare, then that reputation gets around. Somebody asks a person on that committee, "Is Frank a good real estate agent?" The response may very likely be, "I'm sure he is. I've never done any business with him but he is very thorough, always follows through and is a pleasure to work with. I'd list my property with him in a heartbeat."

I'll give you a, "for instance." One of the gentlemen in my local chamber got involved in the youth leadership program. He really enjoyed working with youths and decided that this was the committee he could do the most good on. After working with youths in the area on a consistent basis, a lot of the parents got to meet him and heard many good things about him from their kids and the other committee members. As he got to know some of the parents, they asked him what he did for a living. When they found out he was a financial planner, a few of the parents asked if he'd be willing to sit down with them and take a look at their financial portfolio. First one set of parents, then two, then three and so on. Was he expecting this to happen? Did he get involved in this committee to try and "get to" the parents? No. He sincerely liked working with kids. The parents got to see him,

REFERRAL GROUPS, CHAMBERS AND ASSOCIATIONS 283

his sincerity, honesty, and hard work. They developed a relationship with him and trusted him. They approached him to help them. He didn't solicit their business. This is what getting involved can do.

4. Not asking for help—one of the chamber's jobs is to help you network. You need to let them know who you would like to network with. If there are certain members of the chamber you would like to meet, don't hesitate to ask a chamber staff member or another member of the chamber for an introduction. When you go to the chamber mixers, you are there to meet people, not to just eat, drink and be merry. You could do that at home. You are there to build relationships with other chamber members. Set a strategic plan for yourself to meet certain people when you go to a mixer. Have the chamber hosts that are there that night introduce you. This is proper, and the introduction serves as an informal referral. Remember, it is the chamber's job to help you create opportunities for doing business with people in the chamber. So go ask for help.

5. Not getting to know the staff—within the first two weeks you are a member of the chamber, you should call and make an appointment to sit down with the chamber president and get to know him or her better. You have paid a fee to be a member of the organization. So call the staff and get to know them better. At this meeting you can ask any questions you have about the organization. Discuss the reasons you joined the chamber and what you are looking to get out of it. See if your goals are realistic and find out how the chamber staff can help you achieve those goals. If you have been a member of the chamber for a while and haven't done this, then do it as soon as possible. This is one of the reasons you paid your membership dues.

PROFESSIONAL AND TRADE ASSOCIATIONS

At their most basic level, associations are formal membership organizations that are established to serve the needs of the members and/or to promote or safeguard the interests of a trade or profession. In addition, there are associations or not-for-profit organizations which exist primarily to raise money for a particular cause, and other associations that provide opportunities for members to get together with others who share their passion for a particular hobby or field of study.

The mission and goals of associations are almost always broader than just providing networking opportunities for members. And people join associations for a variety of reasons, such as: to "give something back" to society or to their industry or profession; to further their personal or professional development; to have a voice in influencing legislative or regulatory bodies; to participate in the establishment of or adherence to certain standards of practice; and so on. In truth, no association with a diverse membership base can be a "perfect fit" for any one member, but every association you join gives you an opportunity to meet large numbers of people with whom you have something in common on which to build a relationship.

By and large, professional societies and associations have individuals as members, while trade associations represent companies. Philanthropic organizations are established to raise money for a particular cause, and foundations provide financial support primarily for educational or research endeavors. Then there are religious, charitable, social, and educational organizations, clubs and associations. In fact, there are more than 1.2 million associations in the United States. Obviously you can't be a member of all of them. So how do you decide which ones to join? Well, the first step is to figure out what you want

REFERRAL GROUPS, CHAMBERS AND ASSOCIATIONS   285

to get out of your membership. For our purposes, let's focus on your desire to develop more business through association networking. In that case, you will want to identify those associations whose mission and goals are most closely aligned with your marketing and sales strategy. Bluntly speaking, join those organizations where you are most likely to: (a) meet people who could become your customers, (b) meet people to whom you would be able to refer business and from whom you could reasonably expect to receive referrals, (c) learn about your customers and/or your competitors, and, best of all, (d) all of the above.

Associations, like Chambers of Commerce and Referral Groups provide you with a number of benefits, including:

A Visibility

 1. for yourself

 2. for your company

B Access

 1. to referrals

 2. to customers

 3. to information

C Opportunities to demonstrate capabilities

 1. of yourself

 2. of your company

 3. of your products and services

D Relationships

   1. to form them

   2. to continue them

   3. to cultivate them

E Learn

   1. about your industry or profession

   2. about your customers, their needs and concerns

   3. about your competitors

To turn your membership in an association into opportunities for networking and business development, you have to be more than just a listing in a membership directory. As with chambers and referral groups, they will work for you only to the extent that you work them. There are a number of ways you can support an association while your efforts work to your benefit. For example, you can:

1 Offer your services to the association on a pro bono basis, which allows you to demonstrate your abilities and style of working and establishes your credibility with the other members of the organization.

2 Contribute some of your products to the association as samples to build exposure and name recognition.

3 Host or sponsor events that are run by the association such as cocktail parties or coffee breaks at conventions or meetings, or offer to provide "giveaways" such as pens, notebooks, tote bags, etc., in exchange for having your company recognized for its contribution by having its name printed on the materials.

REFERRAL GROUPS, CHAMBERS AND ASSOCIATIONS

Doing so presents an image of scale and substance to your company, and it builds credit for you with the leadership of the organization.

4   Utilize the association's resources. For instance, you might be able to rent its mailing list if you're looking for direct access to individuals; you could have a booth at the association's trade show; or you could advertise in its publications. Remember to make sure you are listed accurately in the membership directory and buyer's guide.

5   Participate in the organization's events, offer to teach or speak at seminars, join committees and task forces, and share information through surveys and reports. Let people know that you are interested in the association and that you want to be involved.

6   Volunteer to serve in leadership positions such as board member or committee chairperson. Actively recruit new members for the association and offer to represent or serve as spokesperson for the organization in public settings. Make other people want to get to know you so they will seek you out and you don't have to look for them to join your network.

Based on our cumulative experience as association executives and as consultants to chambers and associations, we have put together a list that will help you.

THE TEN COMMANDMENTS
OF ASSOCIATION NETWORKING

I   Thou shalt not confuse introductions with invitations.

II   Thou shalt not use volunteer service as a subterfuge for personal gain.

III   Thou shalt not assume a relationship exists simply because you are a member.

IV   Thou shalt not act as though the association exists solely for your benefit.

V   Thou shalt not equate simple exposure with effectiveness.

VI   Thou shalt stay focused on the strategic issues.

VII   Thou shalt be subtle, but not shy.

VIII   Thou shalt seek leadership positions for the good of the whole organization.

IX   Thou shalt be consistent in thy message.

X   Thou shalt be responsive to referrals given to you, and to those sought from you.

Chapter 19

INTRA-NETWORKING

CROSS-SELLING—AN ELUSIVE GOAL

As noted earlier, on the surface many companies appear to have significant opportunities to develop large amounts of new business simply because one group or part of the firm is able to refer work to other divisions. The big accounting firms come to mind immediately: their well-entrenched audit partners feed leads and work to the consulting groups. In theory, it seems like a clear-cut competitive advantage; in practice it is rarely that easy. In our interviews with different

SUCCESSFUL BUSINESS NETWORKING

types of firms, they offered many reasons why cross-selling fails to live up to its potential, including:

○ One person or one part of the company that already has a relationship with a customer doesn't want to jeopardize that relationship by bringing in another person or practice area which may do something that could anger or alienate the customer.

○ Those persons responsible for business development in one area are often too busy with their own responsibilities to have time to look for opportunities for another group.

○ Many managers tend to wear "blinders" and can only see or hear opportunities for their own areas of responsibility; frequently they are not even aware of all the products or services their firm offers.

○ Most firms offer no incentives to those who bring in business outside of their own practice area or line of business.

A few companies, however, have been able to overcome these obstacles to cross-selling. Here are some of their secrets:

○ Education and reinforcement of the importance of cross-selling to the firm's culture and to the individual's future with the firm must begin upon employment and continue throughout their time with the firm.

○ Tracking and disseminating information about all of the company's products and services and the personal capabilities of each member of the company's employees is crucial. In many larger organizations, an individual has been designated and given both the responsibility and the authority to function as the firm's "knowledge development officer."

○ Encourage staff members to establish internal referral networks among the company's employees and reward those individuals whose referrals lead to new business for the firm.

○ Run in-house seminars to teach networking skills and how to apply these skills within the company.

○ Use teleconferences to share information among and between offices and practice areas about the types of customers different groups are seeking.

○ Assign a "Relationship Manager" to each major customer. This person is responsible for making sure that that customer is kept happy as well as for informing the customer about all of the firm's lines of business which are available to meet the diverse needs of that customer.

By and large, the most successful companies are those that have been able to convince their staffs that they are part of a team, not a group of individuals, and that when the team wins, they all win. The tips and techniques we have presented in this book can be as readily applied within your company as they can between yourself and any of your other networking groups. Think of all of the people who work for your company as potential members of your Primary Network, and treat them accordingly.

Part VIII

MAINTENANCE

SECRET 7:

YOU CAN'T CATCH A FISH
WITH A TORN NET

NETWORKING TOOLS: NO-TECH

KEEPING IN TOUCH THE OLD-FASHIONED WAY

No matter how advanced we all become with technology, everyone misses the old days of talking to a real person on the phone, receiving a hand-written letter and not having to press a button to bypass the menu before speaking to who we want. However, technology is "cool." It allows us to be more productive, professional, and, for small entrepreneurs, to appear bigger than we are.

With all this technology, why is it that we are impressed when we get a hand-written note from someone? Because it is not the norm? Because it takes more time than punching a key on your computer to send out a generic letter with names from a database? Yes, to both.

It is important to keep in touch with your Networking Associates on a regular basis, especially those in your Secondary Network. If someone is in your Primary Network you are already in contact with them on a regular basis. That is why you consider them part of your Primary Network. The people in your Secondary Network are the most important ones for you to touch base with regularly. They know you well and will refer business to you consistently if they hear from you.

The no-tech way of keeping in touch is quite simple. Make a phone call, write a letter, have breakfast, lunch, dinner, drinks or coffee. This is the most personal and the strongest way to continue to build your relationships and keep yourself in the forefront of your associate's mind.

First, schedule a time to make marketing calls to your Networking Associates. These are marketing calls because when you are with your associates, you are always marketing yourself. You could have a two-hour lunch with your associate, never speak about yourself and still consider it a successful marketing lunch. Why? Because by contacting your associate you are marketing yourself. Don't underestimate the importance of getting together, talking on the phone or just taking time out for each other.

When you get together with your associate, you should have an agenda of issues to cover. The time you spend together needs to be as productive as possible. With a growing network, you may not be able to get together with this person again for quite some time, so when

NETWORKING TOOLS: NO-TECH

you do get together you need to be sure that you have both benefited from the experience. You have two primary objectives when you sit down with your associates:

1   Find out more about them.

2   Let them know more about you.

We suggest that before you meet for lunch you take out your associate's F.A.B.U.L.O.S. profile card. Read through it and make note of the missing or weak parts of their profile. What is it you really need to learn more about? Write down specific questions. You don't want to refer to this card or read off questions, but use the notes to remind yourself of what to ask during the conversation. The stronger your profile, the easier it will be for you to find some business for them, send some interesting notes or articles to them, etc.

Your second goal is to let them know more about you and your business. Sit down and think about what you have discussed with them in the past and what specific things you would like them to know now. Vary the information. This makes a more interesting conversation. Let them know more about you, personally and professionally.

This type of continual maintenance to your net is the most productive. It will let you deepen your relationships with your networkers. Thus you will be able to move more networkers up in your networking categories and, over time, you will obtain more complex referrals.

Chapter 21

NETWORKING TOOLS: LOW-TECH

IF YOU WANT TO KEEP IN TOUCH, STAY IN TOUCH

You won't be able to have lunch with all of your Networking Associates, nor will you be able to call all of them. But you should be able to contact them all on a regular basis. You need to keep in touch with your Dormant, Inactive and Mailing List networkers, even though you don't get much, if anything, from them, because the unwritten rule in networking is, "You never know."

You never know when you are going to run into one of these people. You never know when they are going to call you, out of the blue, to do some business with you. You never know who they know. And you never know when they are going to refer you to that big client that you never knew they knew. You Just Never Know.

This is when technology really starts to pay off. If you have the technological capabilities, you have many options to keep in contact with these people. Some of your choices are: database generated letters, newsletters and broadcast faxes. All of these are easy to do with a desktop or laptop computer and the right software programs. This type of contact should become part of your regular schedule, but you only need to do this about once every three months. These options allow you to contact many networkers at once and give them all the same message.

Database Generated Letters

Customized and personally addressed database generated letters are generic letters you can send to all of your networkers. The letter won't begin, "Dear Networker," but "Dear John." The point of writing a letter in your database program is that you only have to write one letter; then you can print as many as you like, personalized to whomever you desire. This is what we call your personalized mass mailing. You can send one mailing to all of your networkers and deliver a personal message. It's a good way to stay in touch.

Newsletters

Newsletters take a little more time and energy on your part but they are an effective way for you to keep in touch with your networkers. An ideal length for your newsletter is one page or two sides of one page. If you design it correctly, it could be a self mailer; then you will save the

NETWORKING TOOLS: LOW-TECH

SMP Consulting, Training & Development
Frank J. De Raffele, Jr.
96 North Ave. - - Beacon, NY 12508 - USA
Phone 914-838-2805 - Fax 914-838-1531 - EMail Fderaffele@aol.com

January 1, 1998

\<Name\>

\<Address\>

\<City\>, \<State\> \<Postal Code\>

Dear \<John\>,

Thank you for your order of last Tuesday; we appreciate new clients, as they are the lifeblood of our business. I am enclosing our latest comany brochure, which describes our capabilities and terms of sale. I think you will find the section on in-house training particularly interesting.

Our regional sales representative, Crystal Slaughter, will contact you next week to set up an appointment. At that time, she can explain our programs more fully and answer any questions you might have.

We look forward to serving you again.

Sincerely,

Frank J. De Raffele Jr.
President

FDR: cs

Enc: 1

expense of an envelope. Any good publishing program or up-to-date word processing program will allow you to create a newsletter pretty easily. Be creative and have a lot of fun with this. A newsletter with graphics is interesting to read and a fun break from the daily grind of work. Think up some catchy titles, thought provoking articles and funny items that will make your Networking Associates look forward to receiving your newsletter.

Broadcast Faxes

If you don't know what broadcast faxes are, you are missing out on a great technological advance. A broadcast fax is like a mass mailing, but much easier. If you have a regular fax machine, however, it may not work. Broadcast faxes are best used through your desktop or laptop computer. The program that we use is WinFax and we like it a lot. What programs like this allow you to do is load your associates' names and fax numbers, plus any additional information that you would like to include. When you are ready to send a broadcast fax, pick the names or groups you want to send this message to, hit a few buttons and walk away. Your computer does the rest. You can send two or 200—as many as you like. The computer will make all the phone calls, connect to the other fax machines and transmit the information. If the fax does not go through for any reason, it will let you know. When you check your fax log, it will tell you when the faxes went through and why certain faxes did not. By the way, you can also instruct your computer to try the same number a specific number of times before it gives up. It's a wonderful way to send messages to a lot of people. We use it on almost a daily basis.

NETWORKING TOOLS: LOW-TECH

> Take a memorable quotation from this article (a pullquote) to pique your reader's interest.

Networker's News

March, 1998   **Volume 1, Issue 1**

Ut wisi enim ad min im veniam, quis nostrud exerci tation. Ullam corper suscipit lobortis nisl ut aliq uip ex ea commodo consequat. Lorem ipsum dolor sit amet, conse ctetuer adipi scing elit, sed diam nonummy nibh euismod tincidunt ut laoreet dolore magna. Ut wisi enim ad min im veniam, quis nostrud exerci tation ullamcorper. Susc ipit lobortis nisl ut aliq uip ex ea commodo .

Lorem ipsum dolor sit amet, scing elit sed diam nonummy nibh. Euismod tincidunt ut laoreet dolore magna aliquam erat.

Adi cing donum my nibh euismod tincidunt ut laoreet dolore. Magna aliquam erat volutpat. Ut wisi enim ad minim veniam,

De Raffele & Hendricks Speak Nationwide

Ut wisi enim ad min im veniam, quis nostrud exerci tation. Ullam corper suscipit lobortis nisl ut aliq uip ex ea commodo con-

Networking Tip of the Month

Ut wisi enim ad min im veniam, quis nostrud exerci tation. Ullam corper suscipit lobortis nisl ut aliq uip ex ea com- modo con- sequat.

Lorem ipsum dolor sit amet, conse ctetuer adipi scing elit, sed diam non- ummy nibh euis- mod tincidunt ut laoreet dolore magna. Ut wisi enim ad

Staskel's Business Development Corner

Lorem ipsum dolor sit amet, scing elit sed diam non- ummy nibh. Euis- mod tincidunt ut laoreet dolore magna aliquam . Ut wisi enim ad min im veniam, quis nostrud exerci tation. Ullam cor- per suscipit lobor- tis nisl ut aliq uip ex

ea commodo conse- quat. Lorem ipsum dolor sit amet, conse ctetuer adipi scing elit, sed diam nonummy nibh euismod tincidunt ut laoreet dolore magna. Ut wisi enim ad min im veniam, quis nos- trud exerci tation ullamcorper. Susc

ipit lobortis nisl ut aliq uip ex ea com- modo consequat. Lorem ipsum dolor sit amet, scing elit sed diam non- ummy nibh. Euis- mod tincidunt ut laoreet dolore magna aliquam . Lorem ipsum dolor sit amet, scing elit sed diam Lorem

PUT YOUR WORDS IN ACTION

Be as creative as you like with your computer—write a letter, do a one-page newsletter, design a card, or make anything else you can think of. When you are ready to send it:

○ Go to File and pull down the menu.

○ Click on Print.

○ When the Print box appears, click on the printer select button.

○ One of your choices will be WinFax (or whatever program you are using). Click on it.

After a few seconds your fax program will come up on the screen and then you can choose who you want to send your document to. You may include a cover page or just leave it blank. Once you've made your choice, click on Send and relax. Your computer will do the rest.

Faxing a one-page newsletter is a unique way to keep in contact with your associates. Most people will read it immediately because a fax has a sense of urgency. Be creative and have fun.

Chapter 22

NETWORKING TOOLS: HIGH-TECH

NETWORKING IN THE 21ST CENTURY

We left a message for Bill Gates to see if he can help us change the term Information Super Highway to Networking Super Highway, and the term World Wide Web to World Wide Network. We'll keep you informed of our progress.

If you haven't surfed the net yet, put down this book, pick up a surfboard and put a mouse in your hand. Talk about exciting things happening right before our eyes. If the Internet is not the ultimate networking tool then I don't know what is. Web pages, e-mails, downloads, live video, interactivity, worldwide relationships, home shopping, business advertising—what exactly is it that the Internet can't do? Not only is this a great way for you to get your message out to people locally, regionally, nationally and globally, but soon you will probably be able to contact and conduct trade with extra-terrestrials from Mars and beyond. We're working on that one with Bill, too.

Seriously though, technology provides a number of ways for you to keep in contact with your networkers. The best way to start is through mass e-mail. This is similar to a broadcast fax, but sending an e-mail allows your Networking Associates to read their mail at their leisure. Everyone has a schedule and sets certain times aside for particular daily activities. I read my e-mail early in the morning and I check it once or twice per day. I have received three-sentence "hello" letters and full 60-page documents. I print out my e-mail if I don't have the time or desire to read it immediately; then I bring it with me and read it later. Once you have your e-mail system set up you can load your networkers' e-mail addresses into your address book. Then at the click of a button you can send mail to a few of them or all of them practically instantaneously.

Another way you can use the Internet is by setting up your own interactive web page. Web pages can be as simple or as complicated as you like. You can set up and design your own for virtually nothing, or you can hire a company to design a simple one for you for about 100 dollars (or you could spend up to 30 or 40 thousand dollars). It all depends on your budget and your imagination.

If you can, design a web page that can be updated on a regular basis. Then let your associates know that every so many days they can log on to your site for new information. If you were to do this and combine it with a mass e-mail campaign to remind everyone in your

NETWORKING TOOLS: HIGH-TECH

network to check out your site, that would work best. You might even want to encourage them to send an e-mail message to you with their feedback.

Your website will be visited by people from around the world. You never know what type of networking opportunities this could open up for you. Many new businesses have been formed because of the Internet and monetarily successful strategic alliances between companies have begun as well.

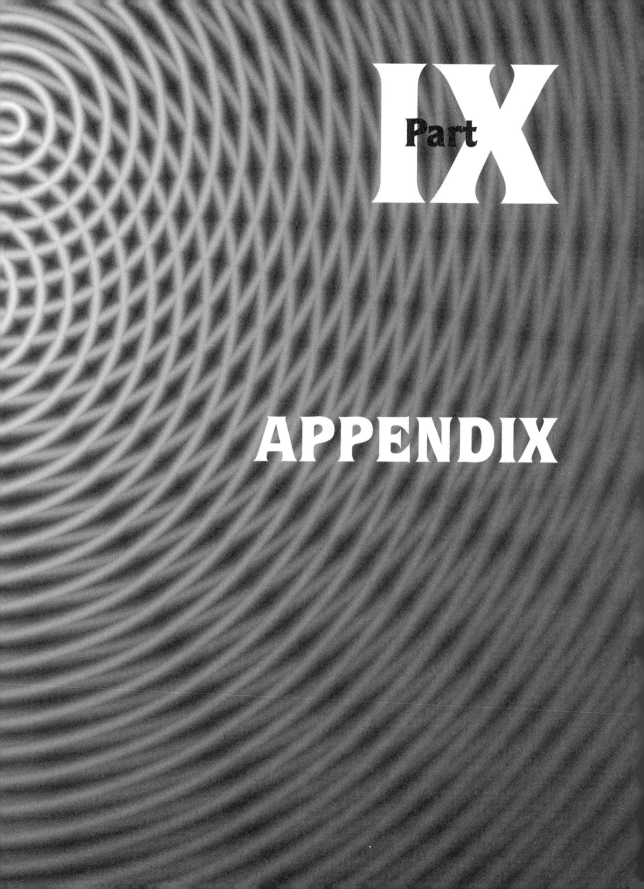

Part IX

APPENDIX

TEST YOUR SKILLS

1 Which of the following are reasons you should network?

   a Personal sales force

   b Diversify your business

   c Polish your sales pitch

   d Important to your career

   e Open a world of possibilities

   f Get ahead of the competition

   g All of the above

2 Networking is synonymous with _____ _____.
(*page 13*)

3 You should update your goals every

   a day

   b week

   c month

(*page 77*)

4 "Take a NAPP and get more referrals." This means that if you lay down in the afternoon you will make more money at night.

True False (*page 91*)

5 The 4 types of help you will get from your Networking Associates are:

1._____ 2._____ 3._____ 4._____
(*pages 92–94*)

6 The 3 levels of referrals are:

1._____ 2._____ 3._____ (*page 95*)

7 What does DBN stand for?

_____ _____ _____ (*page 117*)

8 Name 3 professions in your DBN:

_____ _____ _____

9 List 3 traits of a Successful Networker:

_____ _____ _____ *(pages 131–137)*

10 Name 5 things your Networking Associates need to know about you:

1._____ 2._____ 3._____ 4._____
5._____

(pages 143–144)

11 A business mixer is where different business people get together and mix their own drinks.

True False (Now answer seriously. *page 159)*

12 Name 2 Networking Tools:

_____ _____ *(page 161–162)*

13 Impression, Interest and Story are all part of:

a Jargon of a bank

b a children's book

c the Rules of "7"

(page 172)

14 List 2 ways Introverts feel and think:

_____ _____ *(pages 183–184)*

15 List 2 ways Extroverts feel and think:

_____ _____ *(pages 185–186)*

16 Name 2 techniques of a good listener:

_____ _____ *(pages 198–199)*

17 What are 2 ways to make customers raving fans?

1._____

2._____ *(pages 233–234)*

18 What are 5 marketing secrets?

1._____ 2._____ 3._____ 4._____
5._____ *(pages 261–272)*

19 Referral groups are the same as Chambers of Commerce.

True False *(page 275)*

20 If you want to make more money join a _____ group.
(page 276)

21 List 2 opportunities to build your business in a chamber of
commerce:

1._____ 2._____ *(page 280)*

TEST YOUR SKILLS 315

22 List 2 mistakes people make after joining a chamber of commerce:

1._____ 2._____ (*pages 280–281*)

23 Intra-networking is the cross-selling of other divisions of your company.

True False (*page 289*)

24 No-Tech Networking Tools are:

a pick and shovel

b phone and handshake

c 2 cups and a string

(*page 296*)

25 Low-Tech Networking Tools are:

a Walkie Talkies

b Newsletters, Broadcast Faxes

c CB Radios

(*pages 300–303*)

26 High-Tech Networking Tools are:

a E-mail & Website

b E-mail & Website

c E-mail & Website

(*pages 305–306*)

SUCCESSFUL BUSINESS NETWORKING

27 Name the 7 Secrets of Successful Business Networking:

1._____,

2._____,

3._____,

4._____,

5._____,

6._____,

7._____.

(first page of book)

28 Name the 7 Fundamentals of Successful Businesses:

1._____,

2._____,

3._____,

4._____,

5._____,

6._____,

7._____.

(page xli)

TEST YOUR SKILLS

317

29 Name the two authors of this book:

_____

_____

(book cover)

30 The most effective way for this system to work is to get all your Primary and Secondary Networking Associates on the same system.

True True

TEST ANSWERS

1 g

2 Building Relationships

3 c

4 False

5 Information, Contacts, Connections, Referrals

6 Simple, Compound, Complex

7 Direct Business Networks

8 Different for each person

9 Any of the 7 that start on page 105

10	Any of the 25 that start on page 120
11	False
12	Any of the 7 Networking Tools on page 137
13	c
14	Any of the 13 on page 155
15	Any of the 12 on page 156
16	Any of the 10 on page 169
17	Any of the 10 on page 199
18	Any of the 60 that start on page 226
19	False
20	Referral
21	Any of the 5 on page 244
22	Any of the 5 on page 244
23	True
24	b
25	b
26	a,b,c
27	There are 5 Categories of Networkers

27 There are 5 Categories of Networkers

Take a NAPP, Get More Referrals

Look Inside before Going Outside

Networkers Are Made Not Born

Help Yourself by Helping Others

United We Stand, Diversified We Conquer

You Can't Catch a Fish with a Torn Net

28 Organization

Evaluation

Research

Skills Development

Sales and Marketing

New Markets Development

Maintenance

29 Frank J. De Raffele Jr.

Edward D. Hendricks

30 True, True

Chapter 24

NETWORKING STORIES OF THE FAMOUS AND NOT SO FAMOUS

MAKE YOURSELF MEMORABLE

Somers White is a Certified Management Consultant as well as a member of the National Speakers Association. In both of these roles, Somers spends a lot of time on the road, traveling all over the globe for consulting assignments or speaking engagements. With such a busy schedule, one might imagine that he has little time to keep in touch with the members of his network. Yet just the opposite is true. Somers is never out of the minds of his associates, because he knows that he can't afford to be.

Every place that Somers and his wife, Susan, travel in the world, he makes sure he has their picture taken—usually at one of the more famous tourist locations. Then he has the photos made into postcards which he mails to each and every member of his Primary Network, and to most of his Secondary Network as well. Somers believes that the old saying "Out of sight, out of mind" is true, and by using photos he not only lets people know what he is up to, he keeps himself in sight as well as in mind. According to Somers, every piece of business he has gotten in the last several years has been the direct result of a referral. People remember Somers because he remembers them and because he differentiates himself from everyone else by sending unique postcards. Make yourself memorable.

WIN FRIENDS AND INFLUENCE PEOPLE

Dale Carnegie wrote his famous book *How to Win Friends and Influence People* in 1936. Over the intervening 60 years, nearly 20 million copies of the book have been sold. This is a testimonial to the realization that effective leadership depends on one's ability to work with and through other people. In fact, research conducted by The Carnegie Institute of Technology revealed that even in technical fields, only about 15 percent of a person's financial success is due to one's technical knowledge, and about 85 percent is due to skill in human engineering—to personality and the ability to lead people. Today, each year thousands of people participate in educational programs run by Dale Carnegie & Associates, Inc. The ongoing success of these programs bears testimony to a man who knew the value of word-of-mouth marketing and taught himself to become an effective networker.

LET OTHER PEOPLE HELP YOU TO THE TOP

If you want to know who the best networkers of all time are, simply take a look at the President of the United States—any President. Some were war heroes and rode the coattails of their battlefield victories to the White House. Others came from a long background of political service—Congressmen, Senators, Governors, etc. Recently, our Presidents have included a movie actor, a peanut farmer, a Senator and a Governor of a relatively lightly populated state. On their own, none of these men knew enough people to get them elected to the highest office in the land. But they reached out to all of their networkers—Primary, Secondary, Dormant, Inactive and Mailing List— and encouraged each of the people on all of their lists to likewise reach out to everybody they knew, and so on. Pretty soon the presidential candidate literally had millions of people who felt that they were somehow connected to him. Because of this sense of connectedness, these voters went to the polls and felt as though they were electing a friend, even though they may have never met the candidate personally. They knew someone who knew someone who had met the President of the United States. As such, they were part of the most powerful network in the land.

REMEMBER THE LITTLE PEOPLE

My Uncle Bill (Hendricks) was a milkman for a local dairy in Connecticut for several years and has been retired now for close to 20 years. I cannot recall a single time going anywhere with my Uncle Bill without running into at least four or five people that he knew by name and who knew him. Uncle Bill said hello to everyone on his milk route, whether they were a customer or not. Today he spends a lot of his retirement time walking to and from the post office, the shopping center, the bakery, etc., and he still says hello to everyone he meets.

More than once I have been the beneficiary of his networks. When it was time to get my driver's license, I went to the motor vehicles office, along with what seemed like 300 other people who were all applying for their license on the same day. It so happened that one of the agents was on my uncle's milk route. When he saw the name Hendricks, guess whose name was called first and who jumped to the head of the line! At practically every speech I have given and at practically every workshop I have run in the Connecticut area, at least one person in the audience comes up to me at the end of the session and says, "I know a guy named Bill Hendricks. Are you related to him?" When I say "Yes," I suddenly have a new ally, and, more often than not, someone to add to my network.

DON'T BE AFRAID TO ASK

Howard Blank had just graduated from college and taken a job as a life insurance salesman with New York Life Insurance Company in 1971. My wife and I got a call from Howard. He said that a friend of ours had given him our name and told him that we had just had a child. Because Howard used my friend's name, I agreed to meet with him, even though I had convinced myself I was not in the market for insurance. By the time that initial meeting was over, Howard had changed my mind, and I had bought the first policy he ever sold. Not only did I buy some insurance from Howard, but he very sincerely

NETWORKING STORIES OF THE FAMOUS

asked if I knew anyone else that he might contact. I gave him the names of a few friends who had recently gotten married or had children, and today Howard is president of Blank Financial Group in New York City. I still have insurance through Howard, and I continue to provide him with names of people I meet because I know that he will never embarrass me by using "strong arm" tactics. But I never would have given him any names in the first place if he had not asked for them.

NETWORKING IS A UNIVERSAL ENDEAVOR

Karol Wojtyla was a parish priest in Poland. He became known for his innovative programs in youth ministry, which brought him to the attention of the Cardinal Archbishop of Warsaw. Despite the fact that Poland was controlled by the Soviet Union and the practice of religion had to be conducted in secret, Father Wojtyla's steadfast adherence to the faith, his great intellect and his personable nature made it difficult for him to be kept a secret. Eventually he had to leave Poland and study in Rome, where his reputation continued to grow in the eyes of the hierarchy of the Roman Catholic Church. After his studies were completed, he returned to Poland and was named a Bishop. His circle of friends and supporters inside and outside of Poland continued to grow, ultimately leading to his being named Cardinal. When Pope John Paul I died suddenly, not long after taking office, the College of Cardinals reconvened to elect a new Pope. The leading contenders for the position were all Italian, but Cardinal Wojtyla's supporters had other ideas. They began to spread the Polish Cardinal's name as a possible candidate, and when the voting was over, the world had a new Pope and the first Pole to ever hold the position. Father Wojtyla went from a simple parish priest to Pope John Paul II, thanks to worldwide (and some would say other-worldly) networking.

THE ABCs OF NETWORKING

Attitude is everything.

Business comes to those who actively pursue it.

Cooperation is crucial.

Diversify your contacts.

Expend the energy required.

Follow up.

Givers get.

Help others, and they will help you.

Identify opportunities and act on them.

Just do it.

Keep in touch.

Luck can be generated.

Make a statement.

Networkers are made, not born.

Opportunities abound.

Power is the product of the application of knowledge.

Quitters never win.

Referrals are what you're after.

Share your expertise.

Thank yous are always appreciated.

Urgency is essential.

Volunteer to get involved.

Work your networks.

X-out disappointments.

You can do it.

Zap your competition by mobilizing your network.

○ **Attitude is everything**. Mom (as usual) was right when she used to say, "You can catch more flies with honey than you can with vinegar." People are naturally attracted to attractive people. You don't have to be beautiful, but if you want people to like you, you have to be likeable. Take a good look at yourself and ask, "Am I the kind of person I would like to be around?"

Having an upbeat, positive attitude is contagious, and upbeat, positive people quite naturally have more friends. While you may find a few people willing to assist you because they feel sorry for you if you continuously walk around with a downcast look and tales of woe, you will find many more people wanting to participate in your network if you can develop the habit of feeling good about yourself and making them feel good about themselves.

○ **Business comes to those who actively pursue it**. Some management gurus talk about the difference between hunters and farmers. They liken those who actively seek out new business opportunities to hunters, while those who are content to harvest the rewards of prior relationships are known as farmers. In any case, we have never yet met a farmer who has not had to sow the fields before reaping the grain. In today's competitive business world there is no such thing as the luxury of sitting back and waiting for your phone to ring or for the next piece of business to find its way over your transom on its own accord. You have to go out and work for every piece of business that comes your way. Putting your personal sales force in the form of your network to work for you means you don't have to go it alone.

○ **Cooperation is crucial**. By their very nature, networks are cooperative ventures. The members agree to mutually assist one another and to help one another in a variety of ways. The key to generating word-of-mouth business is mutual support. The members of your network might be your friends, but friendship is not the ultimate determining factor in the success of your network. Cooperation is.

- **Diversify your contacts**. As we noted previously, chances are that your friends tend to share a set of common characteristics with you. They are probably by and large of the same race, socio-economic status, etc. In other words they tend to look just like you. Your network, on the other hand, should be composed of people and professions who could open new markets for you and refer business to you and for whom you can do the same. The greater the diversity in your network, the greater the opportunity to gain business from additional sources.

- **Expend the energy required**. You will notice that a key component of the word "network" is "work." To be an effective networker does require a certain amount of effort. Not only are there meetings to attend where you will have an opportunity meet new people, but there are also phone calls to be made, notes to be written and lunches to be arranged between you and your networkers. Also, don't forget that just as your networkers are part of your personal sales force, you, likewise, are a part of theirs. When you are meeting with your customers or prospects, you are expected to keep your eyes and ears open for opportunities for other members of your network, just as you hope they are doing for you.

- **Follow up.** When one of the members of your network provides you with a referral or makes an introduction on your behalf, he or she is placing his or her reputation on the line. Never, I repeat, never damage their reputation by failing to follow up on the referral. Also don't forget to acknowledge the person who provided this opportunity. Keep them informed of your progress, and let them know the results of their efforts.

THE ABCs OF NETWORKING

○ **Givers get**. If you want to get good referrals, you have to be willing to give good referrals to other members of your network. A network is a fairly small and closed community. There is no room for selfishness, and you will soon find yourself on the outside looking in if you are perceived as someone who constantly takes. In networking it truly is better to be a giver rather than a receiver. Don't worry about quid pro quo. If people recognize you as someone who is willing to give more than you receive, you will get more than your fair share of referrals, and chances are the referrals you do get will be good referrals.

○ **Help others, and they will help you.** Most networks provide their participants with more than just business opportunities. If you let others know that you are interested in their personal lives and are willing to help them in any way you can, they will do the same for you. For example, we have been put in touch with travel agents who are able to assist us with our vacation plans (and save us money besides) through one of our business networks. Likewise, we have been able to find doctors in foreign countries, tickets for sporting events that were supposedly sold out, and we have even been able to visit with family members and friends of some of our networking partners during the course of our travels. Getting more business may be the primary purpose of your networking, but it doesn't have to be the only purpose.

○ **Identify opportunities, and act on them**. Throughout the course of this book we are providing you with a number of tips and techniques that work, but they work only if you act on them and put them into practice. In the same way, when an opportunity presents itself or when you receive a referral from one of your network partners, act on it. There is nothing quite so worthless as a wasted opportunity.

- **Just do it**. A famous sporting goods manufacturer made the slogan, "Just do it!" the mainstay of its marketing campaign. As a would-be networker, you would do well to pay heed to that advice. If you want to start networking, the answer is to get started. Sure you'll make mistakes along the way (hopefully, the advice contained in this book will help you prevent or at least overcome some of the mistakes), but if you don't get started, you never will develop your networking skills. The only true failure is the failure to get started.

- **Keep in touch**. "Out of sight, out of mind" is another adage which holds true when networking. If you want your name to be given out as a referral by the members of your network, they have to remember your name. They also need to know what you're up to as far as new products and services that you have to offer. You need to be in touch with every member of your network at least once every six months, not only to let them know about you, but to find out what's new with them as well. It is very embarrassing to be speaking with a member of your network and ask how their wife or husband is, only to find out that the divorce was effective a year ago. Send cards and notes, not only at the major holidays, but every once in a while during the course of the year as well. "Keep in touch" is more than another way of simply saying goodbye. It is a principle component of an effective networking campaign.

- **Luck can be generated**. Some people seem to be born lucky. These are the people who can buy a single ticket and win the lottery. For the rest of us, luck is something that we can have if we are willing to work at it. That's right, you can generate luck. How? By applying the following formula:

Opportunity + Persistence + Practice = Luck.

Other than pure "dumb luck," luck is a matter of identifying opportunities, pursuing those opportunities persistently, and practicing your skills (both innate and those you have learned through education) vigorously. Highly effective networkers are lucky because they work at being lucky.

○ **Make a statement**. When certain people enter a crowded room, they seem to have such a commanding presence that conversation ceases and all attention is focused on them. On the other hand, most of us are not like that, but that doesn't mean that we cannot make a statement about ourselves. The way we dress says something about who we are. The way we carry ourselves can exude an air of confidence. The way we speak can make people want to listen to us. Our marketing materials (brochures, business cards, letterhead, etc.) can make others want to do business with us, or they can have the opposite effect. It is entirely up to you whether you attract other people or turn them away. Make a statement that causes other people to want to be part of your network just because you're you.

○ **Networkers are made, not born**. While it may be true that some people are by nature more effervescent and outgoing than others, it doesn't mean that they are necessarily better at networking. Introverts may have to force themselves to meet people, whereas extroverts seem to have an easier time making acquaintances. As we have pointed out, however, there is a big difference between networking and making friends. By following the tips and techniques provided in this book, even the shyest person can become a top-notch networker.

○ **Opportunities abound**. There are networking opportunities everywhere for those who are willing to keep their eyes open for them. Among the more common groups are: alumni associations, golf clubs, health spas, neighborhood associations, etc. This list does not even include business groups such as: chambers of commerce, trade associations, formal networking clubs, and so on. The list is virtually endless and is limited only by your willingness to explore.

○ **Power is the product of the application of knowledge**. The old adage, "Knowledge is power," is not as true today as it once was. Having knowledge is no longer sufficient. You have to put that knowledge to use. In this book, the authors have attempted to share their experiences and expertise; however, simply reading this book will not make you an effective networker unless you apply what you have learned.

○ **Quitters never win.** We have said it before, but it bears repeating. Effective networking takes work. There will be days when you just don't feel like attending that association meeting or going to that mixer sponsored by your local chamber of commerce. Successful networkers, however, realize the importance of persevering even when they feel like giving up. Your next good referral or piece of business may be waiting for you with the very next person you meet. If you quit before you meet this person, you will have lost before you've begun. Many people

THE ABCs OF NETWORKING

succeed where others have failed simply because they have shown up.

○ **Referrals are what you're after**. Remember, networking is not about making friends. It is not even necessarily about having people tell you about potential new business. What you want are referrals—people who are willing to go out of their way to market on your behalf. You want them to be in a position not just to introduce you to prospective customers, but to "presell" you and your services by giving you testimonials and, to a large extent, by staking their reputations on your ability to do the job for which they are referring you. Sure, several members of your network are likely to become your friends as well as your business partners, but you can't afford to lose sight of the fact that business is what a business referral network is all about.

○ **Share your expertise**. To be an effective networker, you can't afford to hide your light under a basket. Before your personal sales force can provide you with referrals, they have to know what you can do. You don't have to be blatant in promoting yourself or your services, but you do have to let your networking partners know enough about you and your experience, expertise and success stories that they will be comfortable talking to other people about you. In many networking groups the participants agree not to solicit business directly from other members of the group. Instead they frequently agree to provide their services at no charge to other members of the network as a means of sharing information about their services. Call it barter if you will, but the fact is, it can be a very effective form of advertising.

- **Thank yous are always appreciated**. While the objective of networking groups is to help one another, this does not mean that saying thank you is not important. If someone in your group refers a piece of business to you, and even if you are not successful in making the sale, it is not only common courtesy but good business sense as well to let the person who referred you know that you appreciate their thinking of you. Depending upon the nature of your networking group and the scope and quality of the referral, anything from a simple telephone call, to a thank you note, to a more substantial sign of your appreciation may be appropriate.

- **Urgency is essential**. The old saw, "All good things come to those who wait," was obviously not coined by a businessperson. Particularly in today's rapidly changing and competitive marketplace, your customers are not likely to wait around for you to decide to act. Today's generation has been raised with a sense of immediate gratification, and your customers expect you to act now. Likewise, when one of the members of your network informs you of a potential piece of business, you have to act on it immediately. If you don't, you can be sure that your competitors will.

- **Volunteer to get involved**. As we have mentioned elsewhere in this book, it is important to join organizations where you are likely to meet prospective customers and/or people you would like to have in your network. Simply being a member, however, is not enough. You can demonstrate your leadership skills and place yourself in a position to be more widely recognized if you volunteer to become an active participant in the organizations to which you belong. Get involved on committees. Become active in the governance of the organization. Help out in any way you can. Make yourself visible in other ways and let people know that they can depend on you.

○ **Work your networks**. We have said it before, and we will say it again and again. Effective networking takes work. Having lots of names in your address book, and even having your name in lots of other people's address books does nothing for you from a business standpoint unless referrals and marketing opportunities result. You have to tap into and mine the resources available in your network. Otherwise, you are simply involved in a popularity contest. Put the information we have provided in this book to work for you, and you will become successful.

○ **X-out disappointments**. Let's face it. Not every referral you receive will lead to additional business for you or your firm. Likewise, not every introduction you make will result in a sale for the person you introduced. You can't afford to focus on the negatives or the business that did not come your way. Instead you've got to be like professional baseball players who have a shot at making the hall of fame if they get a base hit only three out of every four times at bat. Remember, as we said before, Babe Ruth is still known as one of if not the greatest home run hitters in the history of baseball. No one remembers the fact that he also struck out more often than any other player. Block out your disappointments and focus on your successes and realize that you will always have another chance at the plate.

○ **You can do it**. Hopefully we have convinced you that you can be an effective networker. The fact that you are reading this book indicates that you have sufficient desire. Add to this a commitment to persevere, plus the application of the secrets this book provides, and you surely can do it. You can be a successful networker. You can take more control of your life both professionally and personally. As we noted above, networkers are made, not born. Turn yourself into a networking expert. You can do it.

○ **Zap your competition by mobilizing your network**. You can be sure that your competition is not going to go out of their way to help you succeed. In today's marketplace it is no longer the strong that survive. It is the smart. By using your networks effectively, you not only have the strength of your group to rely on, but you have the cumulative knowledge and experience of your network affiliates. You can zap your competition by mobilizing a personal sales force to engage in a word-of-mouth marketing campaign on your behalf. Networking is the key not only to success but to survival.